Between The Covers

Photograph by Dick Sander.

Between The Covers
The Lady's Own Journal

Lenore Hershey

COWARD-McCANN, INC.
New York

For my team: Sol, Jane, Steve
and Barbara

Library of Congress Cataloging in Publication Data

Hershey, Lenore.
    Between the covers.

    1. Hershey, Lenore.   2. Journalists—United States—
Biography.   3. Ladies' home journal.   I. Title.
PN4874.H474A33   1983   070'.92'4 [B]   82-22091
ISBN 0-698-11226-1

Printed in the United States of America

CONTENTS

PREFACE

Going the Distance

In the chancy roulette of life, occasionally that whirling ball does fall into the right slot. Very early, my chips were stacked in the square marked women's service magazines. Fate's spin was generous, and the number came up.

My beginning years were spent as my parents' only child and the sole girl in a charitable all-boys' camp in upper New York state. Surrounded by small active males with roughcut manners, who played sweaty games that shut me out, I felt both unique and lonely. Fortunately, I loved to read, and there was a library filled with musty classics donated by wealthy nonreaders. I also wrote poetry, banal though not totally trite verse about sunsets and April winds and buttercups in the meadow. Not about passion; that came later.

For a solitary child, building an identity is a do-it-yourself project. I was short on components: no peers, no friendly family structures besides my own to observe, no neighborhood to roam. Then one day, on a magazine rack in the back of Palen's Drug Store on Cold Spring's Main Street, I discovered women's magazines. There they were, big and glossy (with the exception of *Good Housekeeping*, which was always in the smaller size), *McCall's*, the now-defunct *Pictorial Review*, and *Ladies' Home Journal*.

9

For the first time, I discovered the romance of ordinary daily living. Here on page after page were idealized families in gracious homes. Every aspect of life was perfectible. Marriages and motherhood could always be made better. Last year's curtains and last night's pot roast were reclaimable. So was a teenager like myself, in turmoil and saddle shoes. I even found out what I was—a *SUB-DEB,* with my own page written by Elizabeth Woodward, teaching me how to handle slipping shoulder straps, sagging self-confidence, and deflating boys. In other columns, the mysteries of sex were so daintily explained that even those remote rites seemed negotiable. Life was a stirring challenge, not *also* for, but *especially* for a girl.

With limitations, of course. It was the age of Vive la Différence. Comparisons like "Men build bridges and women build the social gaps that leave men floundering" boosted the premise that the little woman who had the grit and cheer to hide her light under a bushel would find her ample reward in the lifelong adoration of a good man. Clinging vines were essential to the architecture of strong marriages. Only the astringent wisdom of Eleanor Roosevelt's frank answers to thorny questions pierced through the roseate haze. Q. *As his wife, do you believe in all the ideas of President Roosevelt?* A. *Certainly not. I am an individual and so is my husband.*

The women's magazines introduced me every month to a whole new rational, upbeat world. But the people who really captured my imagination and fired my ambition were the two co-editors who ran *Ladies' Home Journal,* a married couple named Beatrice and Bruce Gould. Pulsating with purpose, the Goulds hobnobbed with presidents and prime ministers all over the globe, knew the present Queen of England as Lilibet, and had Sunday night supper in palaces and on front lines. They were always so sure, so joyous, so firm in their opinions about everything. ("We like nice voices. We like red-haired people. We dislike people who have goodwill only for persons in their own social set.")

Like sharp winter sunshine, the Goulds' midwestern initiative shone forth from every page. In their minds, the distinct calling of women's magazines was to raise even further the standards of excellence among those who appreciated niceties: the upper class. And, of course, to perpetuate the image of women as nurturers and comforters, raising well-behaved children and propping up adorable men. ("Never Underestimate the Power of a Woman" was developed for *Journal* advertising in 1941, with cartoons showing how women subtly led men to the right decisions.)

To their credit, the Goulds also had a tilt toward larger issues and thought-leaders of substance. They gave a platform to Eleanor Roosevelt, Dorothy Thompson, Walter Lippmann. Their enduring public affairs editor, Margaret Hickey, who later became my own friend and confidante, ran important surveys and symposia on major topics of interest to women. They started a crusade on syphilis and helped to get an anti-venereal bill through Congress. And the Goulds also had elegant taste in authors and books. They published J. P. Marquand, Isak Dinesen, Pearl Buck, Daphne du Maurier, and others from the top literary ranks of the time.

To a girl enthralled with women's magazines, the Goulds' career was a natural role model. Others at my age ached to be movie stars. To me, the Goulds had the ultimate mix of work and adventure. Whenever I relate the following fact, I am usually faced with cynical disbelief. But this is the truth. One day, sitting on the grass at camp, I told my visiting friend Ethel (who today remembers the conversation and will sign affidavits of confirmation) that I had two major goals. One was to own a leopard coat. The other was to be editor of *Ladies' Home Journal*.

The first was a possible; the second was a long shot. I was definitely not midwestern, there was more rye bread than upper crust in my background, and I was not convinced my voice was nice. I was somewhat vague, as a matter of fact, about what editors did when they weren't zipping around from Paris to New Delhi. But I was willing to learn.

Leopards became endangered, and I later settled for mink. But the second wish did come true. Luck, as we self-effacing females are wont to say, was a major part of it, as was social change. But let us not rule out talent and hard work.

I grew up as a human being, a writer, and then as an editor. War and other upheavals altered the role of women in our society, widening their minds and their options. The working woman became part of the culture landscape. Domesticity was no longer the only respectable end for a daughter. The changing ownership and management of the top publications brought in fresh faces and new ways of doing things. I developed my skills, enlarged my Rolodex, and made the most of every opportunity. I found people who believed in me and some who didn't (who provoked me into trying harder). And I was fortunate enough to ride in on the wave made by the pioneers of the women's movement.

I got there. Through women's magazines at their peak, I gained a very special ringside seat on the world, a place to perceive the changing scene, to sample the tastes, textures, and trends of my times.

As senior editor of *McCall's*, then managing editor, executive editor, and finally editor-in-chief of *Ladies' Home Journal* for eight productive years, I was in the swirling center of it all. World events, the pageant of people, excitements in fashion, beauty, decorating, the new food discoveries. New lifestyles emerging with a revolution in values and standards. Big literary properties zooming into the megabuck stratosphere. Personality journalism blossoming, paving the way for *People* magazine and other celebrity publications.

I lived through corporate power struggles that make *Dallas* look like *Pollyanna*. I watched while strong men tripped on their own egos and weaknesses. Why do so many men have this thing about size—the big office, the big title, the big car, the big illegible signature they think is so snappy? Don't they realize that in business, as in sex, size isn't everything—and it's always nice to recognize the name?

Some say that women's magazines are the dinosaurs of the future. As I write this, the *Journal* has come through still another sea change, and I am sure it will survive. I myself have moved from magazines into the brave new world of electronic technology: TV, cable, videotex. But I believe the electronic cottage will still have women's magazines on the table or next to the bed, although they may look different and speak in different tones.

I do know that the three decades I spent on these books gave me a very special vantage point on the passing parade. I saw it happen. The rise and growth of the women's movement, the two-paycheck family. Discos, jogging, yogurt, Pac-Man. Space shots, test-tube babies, food processors. Minipads and cosmetics for men. Chromosome-splicing, satellites, word processors. Massage parlors, X-rated films, *Saturday Night Live*. "Recreational drugs," another term for people-processors, turning human beings into mush.

They were hectic, compressed, hard-working years. But I managed to weave in a full personal life that gave me the emotional operating base that made the whole thing come together. I married my husband, Solomon G. Hershey, when he was finishing his internship in New York after graduating from the New York University School of Medicine. He entered his residency in anesthesiology, a specialty in which he has been a leader all his life. We achieved that rare good fortune, a sturdy lifelong marriage, befitting the woman who in 1954 invented the concept of "Togetherness" as a promotion slogan for *McCall's*. We raised a daughter, Jane, and now she too is juggling a career and marriage. (And I have a son-in-law, Steve Cuozzo, to boast about.)

I have been through all the seasons and cycles of family relationships, the passionate heights and the low arid stretches. Illness and crisis have not been strangers. I have a chronically troublesome leg from an old taxi crash. Parents have been stricken, have suffered, and are gone. The milestones for myself seem to have accelerated; time cannot be bullied. Death seems less of a rumor and more of a reality as obituary pages every day strike closer to home. But I can beat back the dark tides of melancholy with positive plans and zestful involvement. I refuse to grow old when there are still so many interesting things to do; when the music is still playing and the party is still fun.

This book was not embarked on as an exercise in self-justification, or a lecture on magazine editing. One person's Memory Lane is another's dead end, and nostalgia, like a lollypop, thins quickly. As a child, I remember kicking off my blankets and murmuring, "It's hot under the covers." Many years later, when the word *cover* became a monthly creative commitment, I discovered that a lot took place under the shiny surface of the identifying face of the magazine. There was the drama and heat generated by the stories themselves: intrigues and secrets and scandals untold. There were personal behind-the-scene encounters that never showed up in print because they were too controversial or too damaging to reveal. Corporately, too, I learned about exposure to the flame, how to build firebreaks, when to walk, not run, to the nearest emergency exit.

14

Yes, it was hot under the covers. Now it's time to fling them off and go public with the life that is my own, in times that I shared with many.

L.H., 1983

ONE

Tell Me About
Your Childhood

Today's juggernaut journalism has escalated the rules of the interview from acceptable snoopiness into a bloodthirsty game of kill-your-mother-but-get-the-story. Nothing is out of bounds; the barriers of taste have crumbled. Last year, one reporter at a press conference asked a senatorial candidate, "Do you think your recent stay in a mental institution will hurt your candidacy?" The reporter was rewarded with a sharp right to the jaw, an occupational hazard I will possibly never share, since I am either too tenderhearted or too timid to go for the jugular. Most of the time.

These days, people in public life have good reason to feel leery about the press. But the public itself should also be suspicious of press secretaries and public relations outfits who want to dab stage makeup on the facts. The pursuit of veracity is still any editor's major obligation. However, as *The New York Times* and the *Washington Post* have discovered to their humiliation, when major feature pieces showed an embarrassment of creative writing, anyone can find himself in hot water. As I once did. I ran an exclusive interview with Pope John Paul II in the *Journal,* by a highly accredited writer, only to discover later that he had patched it together from snatched words and written statements. The affair blew over quickly because there were indications that the Vatican press officials had helped him somewhere along the line.

I am a cat to whom curiosity is cream. But I believe there are times when interest in humans takes precedence over human interest. True, there can be overlap. Which leads to my confession that I have an interrogation maneuver of my own. *I probe childhoods.*

No surgical training is required. True, there are those who for status or self-protection pull down the veils and refuse to share their vital statistics even with *Who's Who.* But most people, given a sincere and sympathetic listener, are all too willing to open old wounds, untie old knots, and let it all hang out. I make no apologies for my delving, besides pointing out that women's magazines make a natural arena for the subject of childhood. But there is more to it than that. Anyone interested in the essential mystery of human beings knows that the real clues are hidden at the beginning of the plot. Peering into childhoods is more than voyeurism. What we see is a reminder of the common weight we all carry, a reassurance that we are not alone in the haunting memory of early experience.

In the case of performers, they're usually psychologically damaged children who never grew up. Their internally generated stress pushes them out there in front of audiences, begging for the love and attention they never got. Like Marilyn Monroe, for example. Or for that matter, like author Norman Mailer, who wrote two books about Marilyn, one a self-styled "fictional autobiography" to fulfill his own boyhood fantasies.

Of course, a great deal depends on how the person is approached for comment. One writer for the *Journal* exerted such warmth on her subjects that they confused her with God, Mother, and Dr. Freud, even though she taped all interviews.

"I thought she was *my* friend," Meryl Streep told me, referring to a quote that was used. After a lecture to Meryl on not confusing journalism with friendship, I admitted that I had edited out some other quotes as an act both of taste and of mercy. Taping such interviews is legal protection, although I dislike anything more than a pen and a small memo pad. Once I did use a tape recorder, on assignment to visit the wife of a new California governor, Nancy Reagan. It was a great conversation, and I took nary a note. Right. The tape wasn't rolling.

Childhoods. So many have been unraveled for me, in intimate conversations, in meetings, on planes. Feminists sharing their memories of mothers drained of identity by domestic drudgery. Black women remembering mothers forced to work outside the home in demeaning jobs. One of my best friends, scarred for life because her mother had witnessed the murder of *her* parents in their bed. Sibling dramas: some idyllic, like my Riverdale neighbors, the Simon sisters, Carly, Lucy, and Joanna, and their remarkable mother Andrea. Other tales of dominating brothers and suffocating sisters. The great pageant of childhood, spread out across the world, a panorama of happiness and suffering. So many stories. A few rise to the surface.

Tony Curtis: A cloudy afternoon in Hollywood, and Tony toured me through his palatial Norman castle on a routine interview for *McCall's*. In the front hallway, examples of his latest art-kick, box constructions he had done himself, in the manner of Joseph Cornell, haunting arrangements of small, incongruous objects in picture-sized box environments, surrealist stage sets evoking deep emotional reactions. One box, I remember, was particularly disturbing in its arrangement of cigar bands and glass eyes. When we returned to the living room to chat, I casually asked if that one had anything to do with his father. That small question was the trigger. He re-

19

leased a flow of confessions that would have filled a Dos-
toevsky novel, with a little left over for Philip Roth. Tony
Curtis became the Bernie Schwartz of his childhood. I heard
about the shrill, interfering mother. The long-suffering father
who did indeed smoke cigars. The brother who was killed
before his eyes. The other brother who became mentally ill.
The afternoon faded, and so did I. I felt as if I had become
caught in a box myself, with poor, troubled Bernie Schwartz,
not this rich, handsome movie star. Finally I left, exhausted. I
never did write up the interview. I had no place to print it,
short of a psychiatric journal.

Or *Carol Burnett.* Again I was working for *McCall's,* on a
Christmas feature I myself had dreamed up called "A Gift of
Love." Yes, Carol, whom I've known since she started in
show business, would be glad to see me. Again, the setting was
opulent. She'd just moved into her new home, and at first
everything was chatty and bubbly and funny, the way Carol
is. Then we settled down into the Christmas story, and she got
teary. The story she told is now known, but this was the first
time she had shared it with anyone in the press. It was the
whole poignant background of her alcoholic mother, and how,
one December, Carol had persuaded her mother to relinquish
her young sister, Chrissie, to save her from falling into a similar addiction. Years later, of course, it was this situation which
encouraged Carol to sue the *National Enquirer* for falsely suggesting that she had been drunk in a Washington restaurant.

Or *Michael Caine.* One day, this British star sat with me in a
New York hotel cocktail lounge. My mission this time was to
urge him to write that short story he'd promised for a long
time. He said that someday he would still do it, and it would
probably concern his childhood. Tell me about your childhood, I said, hoping it might stir him to action. So he did, for
an hour. I heard about his mother, a cleaning woman, and his
father, a Billingsgate porter. He told me how he had been sent

to a foster home during the British bombings, and how he had been abused until he was rescued by the National Society of Prevention of Cruelty to Children, a charity he still supports. I heard him speak with anger of canings by a cruel headmaster in a school he attended. In his jaunty cockney tones, I recall him repeating the motto his mother had given him: "Be like a duck: calm on the surface, paddling like hell underneath." I wrote that down. But I never got the short story. And I never could adopt the motto for myself. I splash too much.

Or *John Springer*, the famous publicist who handled press contacts for such titans as Elizabeth Taylor, Richard Burton, Henry Fonda, and hundreds of other stars. Only recently, he told me a story about himself that almost broke my heart, although I've known John for years. Nearsighted as a small child, he never could see the movies he still loves so because he sat in the balcony with his parents. When he started to wear glasses, he naturally had them on at school. A harsh teacher, a nun, teased him in front of the second-grade class as "Mr. Four Eyes" and "Harold Lloyd." His classmates took up the torment. Then a dumb doctor, believing himself to be out of earshot, told someone, "This boy will be blind before he is twenty-one." It was only when John passed his twenty-first birthday (he's a hop and skip beyond it now) that he had the courage to confide his pent-up fears and humiliation to his loving wife, June.

Childhood. Anyone here remember Victor Herbert? "Toyland, joyland, beautiful girl and boyland." What an irony in the 1980s, when the toys are electronic space games and the kids are experimenting sexually before they're out of the sandbox, and when "joyland" probably means something you smoke or sniff. And yet, blue-jeaned and tough-talking, they are still children, with needs for love and reassurance programmed into the tissues of their bodies. The children of the Me Generation will also grow up. Whom will they blame for their problems? Drug-pushers, parents, the System, TV, school? All of the above. But never Me.

21

In labyrinthine memories, my own childhood unfolds. It begins with my parents. My father, Max Oppenheimer, was a social worker, a committed humanitarian who was awkward about his own emotions. For thirty-six years, his job, his obsession, was running Surprise Lake Camp for underprivileged boys in Cold Spring, New York, where he was a beloved dictator. At the start, SLC was a year-round institution, with public school classes in the winter months. Then it became just a summer camp, a major institutional undertaking which handled up to five hundred boys on two-week vacations.

Shortly after I was born, we all moved to his assignment. The camp was seven miles away from the nearest community, on a mountain lake near the Hudson River Valley. It was beautiful, but bleak in the harsh winters. To my pretty, sociable mother the seclusion must have been confining, if not imprisoning. Using her previous skills, she became the camp bookkeeper, and turned their one-room quarters into a cretonned family home.

On me, she focused overweening attention, getting A for effort and a gold star for vigilance. That she gave me dependence instead of wings, fears instead of self-confidence, was a reflection, I am sure, of her own anxieties. Later, as a teenager hungry for joy and challenge, I used to feel that my pragmatic, nontouching mother was, in the words of poet Louise Bogan, "one of those women with no wilderness in her heart."

Much, much later, I revised my estimate. Pettiness became fortitude as she nursed my father through tragic illnesses and then faced up to her own battle with the crippling indignities of Parkinson's disease. Perhaps her own wildernesses had always been there, with gates that were locked. Perhaps in a different time, with more options, she would have branched out more, and there could have been a more mutually helpful connection between us. Today, I regret that I cannot reach back to tell her this.

Not that I don't have cheerful memories of those early years. Skating on the snow-cleared lake, cuddling generations of new kittens, going on picnics to West Point and up the tram to Mount Beacon, and being slightly spoiled by everyone as the camp's only small child. And learning. My first piano lessons were from a busboy, Joey Bushkin, and should have had a more lasting musical effect, considering that he went on to be one of the nation's top jazz pianists. Family lore has me reading at three, sitting in with the winter boys at their regular classes. When I was six, my mother decided to move with me to New York City for what is now called more normal socialization. My father arranged to commute as often as possible.

The arrangement was odd, but there was no family rift. In those days, parents did what was best for the children and structured their personal and sex lives around what they had to do.

The city, with its apartment buildings, its traffic, and its impact of people, was threatening to me, and I remember checking every day to make sure I could pick out my window from all the others on the fourth floor. I seemed to have some natural integrative powers, though, because I entered P.S. 26, made friends quickly with both boys and girls, and had birthday parties that were considered the best on University Avenue. Because of my headstart training, I was something of a prodigy at school—in everything but sewing. I flunked potholders, did badly in aprons, and still hear Miss Jennings' rough-edged whine when I pick up a needle and thread.

Living in the city allowed me to become acquainted with my mother's clan, in which she stood out like a practical petunia in a flamboyant bed of passionflowers. For example, my very Chekhovian grandfather. Small, precise, with pincenez and sparse goatee, he had emigrated from Russia in the 1880s to avoid conscription. One of the few Jewish boys in

Petrograd with a gymnasium, or high school, education, he had almost complete recall in Russian of the works of Charles Dickens, a favorite in that country. To learn English, my grandfather spent hours in the reading room of the New York Public Library, studying Dickens in his new language until he became proficient enough to be a Prudential insurance agent. Up until his death, my grandfather's ordinary pronouncements, as well as his many gadfly letters to the *New York Sun*, rang with the rhythms of *David Copperfield*.

My mother had two brothers and a younger sister. Uncle Eli started as a runner in Wall Street, became a stock promoter, stumbled on a man who had a new metal called aluminum, and installed his wife and two daughters in a Central Park West penthouse. Uncle Leo was something else. He wasn't in Wall Street, and he certainly wasn't in social work. He was Damon Runyonesque, a partner in the then-famed Club Richman, and involved in many deals of the speakeasy culture. Raffish, clever, he always wore a Borsalino gray fedora; I had the impression he had something to do with tennis. Because after I went to bed, I would hear my mother pleading with him to stay away from the rackets.

He brought us interesting gifts, some of them in bottles. One day he arrived with a large package and said, "Lenore, this is for you and your future." It was a brand-new typewriter. My mother remonstrated and begged him to take it back. Later, I realized she knew it was "hot" and I guess she was horrified at having anything stolen in the house, just as she later upbraided me for telling someone we had bought a rug on Macy's new Cash-Time plan.

But she gave in, and I kept the machine. I taught myself to type, two fingers, hunt-and-find (which is still my method). I used the typewriter for years, often wondering what important gangster had been deprived by my gain.

Most influential on my life was mother's sister, Aunt Grace.

A tiny, vivid woman with intense eyes and carbon-black hair she wore in bangs, she was a rebel, a freethinker, and above all, *a writer*. She also turned out to be, in many ways, my most significant role model.

Her full name was Helen Grace Carlisle, and eventually she wrote six novels, most of them best sellers, including *Mother's Cry*, which was made into a movie starring Dorothy Peterson and David Manners. Grace had gone to Alfred University, became a Quaker, and worked as a maternity nurse in a Quaker hospital in France during World War I. She went on to Paris, where she started her first novel, *See How They Run*, and mingled with such Left Bank stars as Ernest Hemingway, Gertrude Stein, and Henry Miller. She had been briefly married to an English novelist, but her first two sons were sired by (a) a Hungarian count who became Helena Rubinstein's art director and adviser, and (b) a famous composer of operas who was half American Indian and whose name I never caught. She barely did, too. There was no pill in those days, and impetuous Grace confided in later years that both children were the result of the briefest of encounters.

Naturally, my mother was aghast at all of this, too. *Nobody* lived like that back then, and her greatest concern was that Grace would kidnap my imagination and somehow convert me to her bohemian, amoral ways. Not a chance. I was grateful that I had an example to follow of someone who made a living by writing, and I recognized her as an original, a woman daring to try and find herself. But I was also smart enough to see beneath the glittering surface to the self-centered limitations. She borrowed incessantly from my hardworking, underpaid father and always forgot to pay him back. And all her colorful alliances seemed to leave her holding the bag (and the baby).

Eventually, she settled down somewhat. She married James Reid, president of Harcourt Brace, had another son, and ruled over a gracious small estate in Stamford, Connecticut. It was a kind of literary salon of the day, and at her fabulous parties I met editors and publishers and got a glimpse of the world I would come to someday on my own terms. I also met some of her remarkable women friends: the outstanding woman doctor who delivered all Grace's children; the blind woman who, despite her handicap, ran a large working farm; her agent, Leah Salisbury, who eventually became my first agent, and many others. I am sure this is part of the reason that I have never felt that seeking a career, even in my time, was anything extraordinary.

Grace divorced Jim Reid, wrote and drifted, and died a few years after my mother did. My husband, my daughter, and I all went to her Quaker funeral in the Friends Meeting House in lower Manhattan. It was in the tradition of Friends memorial meetings. Everyone was welcome to speak as an act of testimony. I sat through several pregnant silences, then took to my feet and made a few halting remarks about how I wished I had seen her during that estrangement year before her death. The service went on. Her ex-husband discussed her books. Others remembered her friendship. Somehow, there was something missing. After a long silence, with my daughter's elbow pressing into my side, I finally rose again. This time, I took twenty minutes. I spoke of her roots, of her passionate desire to live life to its full, of her inability, ever, to count the costs. I voiced my gratitude for her encouragements and inspiration, and ended by presuming on her adopted religion and venturing the guess that she had somehow captured the Inward Light in which Quakers put their trust. Afterthoughts are always uncomfortable. At least, this service gave me the chance to vocalize mine.

One other small memory of the Stamford days reappears now and then. On one of my weekend visits, Grace drove me over to a neighboring family: the Tarchers. Mrs. Tarcher was also a career woman, a prominent lawyer, and her husband was an advertising man. They weren't home, but a chic little girl in riding clothes was sitting on the fence. She was a few years younger than I, but my aunt introduced us. The chic little girl grew up to be Judy Krantz, author of *Scruples, Princess Daisy,* and *Mistral's Daughter,* and eventually a good friend. She says she can't remember it all that clearly, reminding me that I am, after all, older.

I have a Kodak snapshot of myself in another car, a white Rolls-Royce. I am about nine, with one of those terrible early perms that makes me look like a mini-Bette Midler. Next to me at the wheel is my first show-biz mentor, Eddie Cantor, the pop-eyed comedian. As a motherless, fatherless boy from the Lower East Side, he had been sent to Surprise Lake Camp by the Educational Alliance. There, he used to say, he saw "the first patch of green that wasn't a pool table." When he later hit the jackpot, he made SLC his favorite charity, running at least one major benefit a year to which all the stars, from Milton Berle to Jack Benny, came and performed.

Every summer he visited camp, causing a furor, and I loved to sit as he regaled my parents and others with his Hollywood stories. I remember him bragging about discovering Dinah Shore and Eddie Fisher, and I also remember him calling his broker at least twice on every visit. He liked to tease me by asking me for my latest poetry, and I'd be the one he'd send for his Boston coolers, a mixture of ginger ale and vanilla ice cream that soothed his ulcer, which was one of many ailments.

I always get a bracing jolt whenever life proves by the linkage of events that maybe it isn't all such a haphazard journey after all. Perhaps I am coincidence-prone, or maybe I have a special deal on time warps. At any rate, like threads that get submerged in the weave and then reappear again, the cast of characters in my life never seems to completely leave the theater.

27

In such vein, the Eddie Cantor story gets picked up further on. Years later, when I first went to work on *Ladies' Home Journal,* the editors were having a kind of flap with Jacqueline Susann, the author, about the photograph they were going to use on the cover of the magazine to herald an excerpt from her newest novel, *The Love Machine.* Jackie Susann at that time was at the height of her celebrity, a showgirl turned writer who rose above the critics' scorn and with the help of her devoted husband, Irving Mansfield, a promotion genius, achieved the role of "queen of kitsch" and ruler of the best-seller lists.

"They'll chew you up," warned my art director, and indeed, both Irving and Jackie (and especially Jackie) had reputations for expletive-studded impatience, which was why I was sent up as a sort of human, soothing Boston cooler.

I took a cab up to Central Park South, and the elevator up to their magnificent apartment overlooking the park. Jackie greeted me alone, except for Josephine, the toy poodle about whom she had written her first successful book, *Not Tonight, Josephine.* The hallway was lined with framed photographs, and as my coat and my inevitable tote bag were being stashed, I noticed one picture of Jackie, young and lush-looking, with an Eddie Cantor of earlier days, about as I remembered him.

"Oh, Eddie," I said. "I knew him when I was a child. My father was the director of Surprise Lake Camp."

The ready-for-battle look on Jackie's face dissolved. We moved into the living room and sat down on a sweeping beige sofa. Josephine took a liking to me and curled up too.

"I adored Eddie Cantor," said Jackie. "He was a very, very special man in my life. Last week we were robbed of all our valuables: furs, diamonds, everything. Do you know what I really wept for? The wristwatch Eddie Cantor gave me back in the forties. Nobody will ever really know how much that meant to me."

The things she told me about Eddie Cantor, that nice family man with his Ida and his five daughters! Eddie, who had also been one of Irving's clients, had obviously been smitten by this adventuresome, dark-eyed beauty who came to Broadway at the age of sixteen in the 1930s. She described his earthiness, his way with a sexy joke, the way he had fostered her career. Jackie's own father, Robert Susan (she added an extra "n") had been a well-known portrait painter, friend of Grace Kelly's father Jack, and at least the fantasy inspiration for the father-daughter love relationship in Jackie's novel *Once Is Not Enough*.

More about Jackie later, because our friendship was cemented that day, and her outspoken, warm dynamism became part of my personal and professional life until she died of cancer on October 21, 1974. I do know that she left me a legacy. When our dachshund died, she insisted that I accept a chocolate-brown miniature poodle puppy from her and Irving. We named him Brillo, and he became a cherished member of the family for thirteen years. Jackie would have appreciated his manner of death. Still eager at his age, he was visiting a local bitch in heat, and two large male dogs attacked him and ripped him to pieces. In his memory, and in Jackie's, we kept the line going when we got another poodle from the same kennel through Mel Davis, Jackie's friend and poodle groomer. The new pup's name is Rovy, and we cherish him.

Childhood. Back to my own, as the storyboard advances to adolescence. I grow. I wonder who I am. I am aware of my Jewishness, but in a detached cultural sense. It takes the Holocaust to awaken me, to stir the identification and pride of heritage which strengthens as I grow older.

I am awakened in other ways. The boys in camp are different: New messages are sent to me by their muscled, suntanned bodies. I have my first real kiss, shut-eyed, toe-tingling, on the floor of a canoe. My mother waits on shore with flashlight, to make sure I don't drown—or worse. Other

29

kisses, other boys, but nothing major happens. I am afraid of my surging feelings, still waiting for the Big Love and the Happy Marriage.

I am educated at the expense of New York City. In elementary school, there's a first prize in an essay contest. At Evander Childs High School, a poetry prize. At Hunter College, a major short story prize. Uncle Leo's typewriter is wearing out. With $75 I get for three winning entries in the *Journal American's* love letter contest, I buy my own machine this time.

I want to work. It is not unusual for the times, the economic frame of reference, or the patterns of my peer circle for me to plan a career. I sell handbags at Macy's, become an editor on a small-town newspaper for one halcyon summer. At Hunter, I major in journalism, and in my last year I serve as a college reporter on *The New York Times*, paid 40 cents an inch for everything I have printed. (I specialize in group listings.) After graduation, I take on a job as an advertising copywriter, first at Macy's, then at an ad agency. My cousin, Joan Angel, joins the WAVES, and I am enticed into ghostwriting a book about her: *Angel of the Navy*. It is a modest success and gets picked up by Twentieth Century-Fox as a possible vehicle for Betty Grable. She jumps ship but I get the salty taste of success. One hot summer weekend, I write a short story in two days. For top dollar at the time, Leah Salisbury sells it to the *Saturday Evening Post*. It is featured on their Christmas cover and turned into a radio program. I pinch myself.

As I move on to the promotion department of the *New York Herald Tribune*, go-ahead signals seem to dominate. I help to run the famous *Herald Tribune* forums, working with Helen Rogers Reid, Irita Van Doren, Clare Boothe Luce. Then, a stop signal. On my way to the *Trib*, a taxi accident smashes my shinbone into fragments. By now, I am married, and my husband and I learn the value of having a partner in crisis. After three months of hospitalization, I am transferred home to a wheelchair, and then to a leg brace. The mirror reflects a defeated me: overweight, despondent, shut off from life. My old boss at the *Trib*, now at *McCall's*, George H. Allen, later to become one of the giants in magazine publishing, asks me to do some free-lance writing at home. I accept instantly. Writing comes easy. Learning to walk takes longer. But it happens. One day, limping slowly, I walk down the halls of *McCall's* to take my free-lance but full-time job. My life on women's magazines has begun. I have found the place to find my place.

Childhood. The further we get from it, the more it becomes exclusively our own. We storm the fortresses of our memories on the psychiatrist's couch, in encounter groups. But the truth is still elusive, even though we may make some minor treaties with our past. Because the truth is that we cannot ever really see how it was with them, those towering figures, our parents. Or with us, the little people who could not evaluate our own— or their—feelings.

Recently, it is a literary fashion for celebrities and their relatives to capitalize on anguished childhoods. There was *Haywire,* by Brooke Hayward, daughter of Leland Hayward and Margaret Sullavan. And, of course, *Mommie Dearest,* in which Christina Crawford, one of Joan Crawford's adopted children, gave her side of what it was like to be the formidable star's daughter—a story which has now been beaten to death with a wire hanger, thanks to the sensationalized movie which was made of the book, with Faye Dunaway playing Joan Crawford.

I have mixed feelings about these love-hate books. Although we did run a biography of Crawford which I retitled *Dark Side of a Star,* I turned down *Mommie Dearest* on the supposition that if Christina's revelations made me squirm, it would have the same effect on readers. I serve as a board member on the National Committee for Prevention of Child Abuse, and the subject is one which needs all the attention it can get, but somehow I felt this was not be the proper ap-

proach. But the broad currency of the Crawford story un-
locked a conversation which I have been carrying around in
my head for years. And because it illustrates that both parents
and children are victims, not only of circumstance, but of their
times, I feel it appropriate to bring it out now.

I call it The Fable, although it is a true incident that happened about thirteen years ago. Eve Siegel, a well-known publicist, asked if I would have lunch with a young soap opera
actress she was representing at the time—the adopted daughter of a high-powered movie star known for her ostentatious
purity. I was eager to oblige, although I suspected I could
never be daring enough to pry out one of the most carefully
guarded stories Hollywood had protected through the years—
the rumored situation being that the "adopted" daughter was
in truth the super-star's own daughter, conceived on location
in the north as the result of a brief affair between the woman
star and Mr. Big, the greatest male lead of his time.

As it happened, I did not have to pry very hard. Not aware
that she was talking to a practicing journalist, the daughter
spilled out a dramatic and convincing narrative of how her
mother had hidden their blood relationship until the daughter
was in her twenties. According to the daughter, she had had a
mysterious cosmetic ear operation when she was five years
old. Her mother had arranged for the surgery in order to hide
any resemblance to the other ears around town. I have all the
words of that vivid, painful conversation imbedded in my
memory. Friends and resources in Hollywood assure me that
there is almost universal acceptance among the senior set of
the truth I was told that day. Yet, because the mother is still
beautiful, socially powerful and politically conservative, because lawyers hover over every threatened desecration of the
privacy of a living legend, and because mother and daughter
seem to have made up their differences, my lips must remain
more or less sealed.

It's a pity. I understand that digging up such long-past liaisons can prove embarrassing. But it's such a human story and so highlights the contrast between yesterday's hypocrisy and today's open standards. It is also a tale of strong and determined women, and of still another childhood that has thrown its shadows over a lifetime.

Perhaps I can turn it into a fictional TV show. That seems to be legally acceptable, although recounting the details of the interview, I am warned, is not.

Childhood. Like sere leaves in an autumn wind, so the remnants of our early experiences spin in our psyches, enriching, haunting, motivating, embittering. Eventually we must face the truth that good parents sometimes have imperfect children, and that failed parents are often acting out their own legacies of alienation and need. In the end, it is only compassion that can save us all. We must grow up inside ourselves as well as in our bones. To understand, to accept, and to forgive are the remedies for both guilt and anger.

Tell me about your childhood.

TWO

Kennedys and Other Legends

In women's magazines, legends are cast not in stone but in warm, vulnerable flesh and blood. It is a style I possibly helped to foster. And it could be gender-related.

Unless they're in Washington or Hollywood, where tattle is legitimate trade news, most men pretend to be above small talk about big names. Women are more honest. They cut right through to the fundamentals on which they have been conditioned to make judgments: personal and interpersonal details. Ask a man if a candidate's profligate private life will affect votes, and you'll get the answer that this does not have anything to do with his public performance. A woman will be more wary. She'll eat up every last despicable detail of the gossip. But she'll also make a moral connection, even if her cynical side tells her that "they all do it."

There are other subtleties. Every good editor views himself or herself as a potential reader and has learned to psych out what is wanted. On celebrities, for example, women readers are ambivalent. They want their heroes and heroines on a grand scale, romantic and true blue. On the other hand, they enjoy magazine pieces that knock halos awry, that reveal the cracks in idyllic marriages, that demonstrate how the pure

35

and the pompous can slip on the banana peels of their own emotions. It's a nice comfortable feeling that ugly things happen to the rich and famous, too.

Magazine editors work both sides of the street. And on dark corners we pause to worry about the supply of personalities. Who will replace those aging Names who are familiar, but no longer surefire? Does a young reader really know or care about Doris Day or June Allyson? On the other hand, is this week's new TV series star worth a big story and a cover? Why, oh why, does there seem to be a shortage of the larger-than-life, towering personalities that we remember from other times? Cover meeting after cover meeting, we wonder how we got caught up in this celebrity bind anyhow, and why don't we really bite the bullet and go to models? However, the star trek stretches on, and somehow the celebrities keep coming through the revolving door.

But in every age there are always a few classics, legends-among-legends that have a continuity of their own and a durability that is persistent. In my book, one name tops the list, uncontested: *Kennedy.* Kennedy stories. Over the years, they have been the bread-and-butter, the caviar and dessert, of women's magazines. Starting with Joseph P. and his wife Rose, peaking with JFK and Jackie, continuing with Robert and Ethel, on through the troubled saga of Teddy and Joan and now into the third generation of innumerable and often untrackable offspring, covers and stories on this quasi-royal family have filled more pages than any other clan. The mother lode was and is mined, and mined, and mined for pay dirt. It still provides a priceless vein for journalists who want to sell copies.

To refresh my memory, I went back over past issues of the *Journal* to see how we handled Kennedy stories over the period of 1969–71. A sampling of headlines:

THE MAN WHO TAUGHT JACQUELINE KENNEDY ABOUT
LOVE AND MARRIAGE, FROM HER COUSIN'S MEMOIRS
(February 1969)

JACQUELINE KENNEDY'S FATHER: HOW HE FOUGHT FOR
HER LOVE (March 1969)

MY BOSS, JACQUELINE KENNEDY, BY HER FORMER PER-
SONAL SECRETARY (July 1969)

THE "SHOTS" THAT CAN SAVE A MILLION LIVES, BY SEN-
ATOR EDWARD M. KENNEDY (September 1969, but
printed before Chappaquiddick)

THE GIRL IN TED KENNEDY'S CAR (October 1969. We got
that story quickly.)

GIVING CHILDREN THE GIFTS OF FAITH AND COURAGE,
by Rose Kennedy (December 1969)

THE NEW YORK LIFE OF JACQUELINE KENNEDY ONASSIS
(February 1970)

AN ACCOUNTANT'S AUDIT: THE $2,000,000 HONEYMOON
OF JACQUELINE ONASSIS (June 1970)

And then, in February 1971, still another Kennedy min-
ion not yet heard from. Washington newshawk Maxine
Cheshire, who stalked Kennedy stories like a bird dog from
her home state of Kentucky, found old Joe Kennedy's former nurse, Rita Dallas, who came up with, among other
things, what Ted Kennedy told his ailing father in her
presence.

"I was in an accident, Dad, and a girl was drowned. That
was all there was to it, but you're going to hear a lot more of
it on TV."

That was one of Ted Kennedy's more astute evaluations.

Actually, these articles were not as superficial or as blatant as they
sound. A long time ago, I made peace with the fact that as part of my
job I was supposed to sell magazines. Not my soul, magazines. My

*soul was bid on from time to time. But in the things I cared about—
excellence, truth, responsibility for both the mental and physical well-
being of readers, and freedom to make my own uninfluenced editorial
judgments—on these, my principles never moved across the counter.*

One gets an uneasy feeling to realize that if John F. Kennedy had lived, he would today be eligible for Social Security. However, as he is perceived through the years, JFK
was the heart and core of the Kennedy legend, the fire-
bearer whose flame was snuffed out by an assassin's bullet
on November 22, 1963. These days, when we are deadened
by what now seems to be a series of terrorist assassinations-
of-the-week, we cannot fully recall the shock and outrage we
felt at the thunderclap of his death in Dallas. JFK himself
once said, "The only two dates that make people remember
where they were are Pearl Harbor and the death of Franklin
Roosevelt." He managed to trump both of these dark aces
and still remains the most painful assassination of them all.

In 1963 I was working at *McCall's,* a senior editor whose
unsigned writing was all over the magazine. I did three
features every month: an entertainment roundup and
cultural review called "Sight & Sound"; a behind-the-
scenes editors' feature called "Living With People"; and
Perle Mesta's party column. The latter was signed by her,
but I ghostwrote it and also helped her plan and execute the
parties. Perle, of course, was the former ambassador to Luxembourg, the "hostess with the mostes'" played by Ethel
Merman in the famed musical *Call Me Madam.* She herself
was a legend for the wonderful parties she gave, and for the
top personalities on both sides of the political fence "Two-
Party Perle" attracted to her home. Perle Skirvin Mesta
had an earthy Oklahoma wisdom (she knew every First
Lady back to Mrs. Wilson) and many White House secrets
which she shared with me until her death in 1975. "The
only President who didn't play around with other women

was Harry," she told me. "I always thought he had a crush on *you,*" I responded, and watched her blush.

On November 21, Perle was invited to host a major reception for 1,500 San Juan socialites at Bob Tisch's Americana Hotel in Puerto Rico. She was allowed to bring a few guests on the house, and her entourage included the mayor of Cleveland and his wife, Ambassador Matsas of Greece, my editor John Mack Carter and his wife, Sharlyn, and my husband and myself. We were all in a festive mood, and the red carpet treatment started at the airport. Just a few days before our departure, John Carter had asked me to handle an assignment for him. Lady Bird Johnson, the Vice-President's wife, was considered to be pretty much of a nonstory at the time. But a very dynamic press secretary named Liz Carpenter was coming to town with a text piece and some pictures to try and interest us. I took her out to lunch at the Four Seasons, laughed at her wit, and savored her chili-sharp Texas observations. But the day before we flew to Puerto Rico I put the story and photos in an envelope with a polite letter of rejection, and mailed them back to Washington, where the Johnsons were living at Perle's former estate.

On November 22, as the second day of celebrations began in San Juan, we all moved on from lunch at the Hotel El Convento to the Casa Blanca, or White House, where the head of the Puerto Rican military resided. As we walked in, he approached us with a somber look and told us that President Kennedy had been shot. The soldiers were down in a courtyard listening to a portable radio, and we finally heard the news in Spanish. I will never forget the scene as we stood in the dark mahogany dining room overlooking the Morro Castle entrance to San Juan Bay, with a bleak shipwreck symbolically foundering in the distance.

"I always knew it!" exclaimed Perle, who was not a Kennedy fan and whose friendship with the Johnsons was strong. "I always said Johnson would be President some day."

It was not exactly tasteful, and I could have throttled her. But that was Perle. As her adviser, I urged her to disappear from the Washington scene until well after the funeral. Which she did.

The party was over. Ambassador Matsas took the next plane, and we all left soon afterward. Like good journalists, however, we held a rump editorial meeting that weekend in New York. John Carter looked at me and asked the inevitable question: "Can you get that Johnson story back?"

The day after the funeral, I was down at the scene I had been watching on the weekend on TV. I found the photographer who had taken some portraits of Lady Bird (I bought them, but we decided to rephotograph), and I reestablished contact with Liz, who became a longtime friend from that week on. In the afternoon, I was allowed to attend President Johnson's first press conference in the Fish Room, where a saddened, resentful group of reporters faced him. One famous blond correspondent in front of me whispered to an associate, "Now all the style and glamour has gone . . . we're stuck with Johnsons and Perle Mesta." A few months later, she was down at the ranch riding around in his car with LBJ.

I was wearing a big black fox hat, I remember, and I kept it on because there was no place to put it. After the Fish Room conference, Pierre Salinger, who had been JFK's press secretary, had a subsidiary briefing in his office, and I trotted along with the crowd. I'll never forget standing in the back of the room and watching a red-eyed Salinger trying to remain professional as he kept saying, "President Ken . . . I mean, President Johnson," over and over again.

He seemed to be staring at me, and after the meeting, I went up to reintroduce myself.

"Oh, Lenore," he said. "I'm sorry I didn't recognize you. All I kept thinking as I looked at you is that someone could come in here with a hat like yours with a gun hidden in it."

After I left the press secretary's office, I spent a few of the most poignantly memorable moments of my career. It was in the West Wing (where Kissinger eventually moved), and by now everyone had departed and the grounds were dark and empty. The nearest security station was down the curved driveway at the gate, and nobody seemed to see me loitering just a hundred feet from the White House, looking up at the one lit window in the private quarters, where Jackie was undoubtedly packing. I stood there for about ten minutes, in my own private ceremony of mourning and continuity, filled with the lonely awareness that all things pass, feeling a sense of communion with all my fellow-Americans who fixed so much hope and trust in this House and its occupants, intoxicated by the prestigious oddity of my brief and unnoticed vigil. Then I looked down and in the grass just inches away from me was a solemn squirrel, on his hind legs, regarding me quizzically. I don't usually talk to squirrels, but I did this night.

"Thank you for letting me stop by," I said, without feeling the slightest bit silly. He ran away, and I continued walking down the driveway to the gate, where Mrs. Johnson's photographer was waiting for me in his big white convertible.

He had a phone in the car. And as he headed toward the airport, I decided to call my boss in New York. It took a few minutes, and I heard John on the line.

"I got everything," I said. "I'll be in bright and early tomorrow."

"Where are you calling from?" asked John.

"From a car," I said. And suddenly I looked up and realized that we were passing Arlington Cemetery on the hill. As I spoke, I could see the flame that was lit over JFK's grave. It was so moving I could not speak.

"I'll tell you about it tomorrow," I said. And for the first time that day, my eyes filled with tears.

The five years between 1963 and 1968 seemed to be compacted in my mind. I was still at *McCall's* in 1968; John Carter had moved on to *Ladies' Home Journal*. I had escalated to the top of *McCall's* masthead as "special projects editor." Technically, the editor-in-chief was James Fixx, who later gave up running magazines to make a career just of running. But the real power was Norman Cousins, that indefatigable, gifted liberal who personally dedicated himself into whipping this faulty society into his idea of a more perfect order. He had expanded his duties on *Saturday Review* to a supervision of *McCall's* so that he could also mold it into a magazine that could awaken women to their larger responsibilities. It was a noble effort, and one of the most stimulating, cerebral periods I ever spent on magazines. Along with a dynamite young woman who had been running cultural affairs for New York City, Barbaralee Diamonstein (today married to Carl Spielvogel, the adagency head), I worked on seminars about the future, black power, violence. But they, and all the brilliantly written editorials, didn't help at the newsstand. Over at the *Journal*, John Carter and his two henchpersons, Peter Wyden and future novelist Lois Gould, were using a hard-hitting, newsy, visceral approach—and it was working.

On the morning of June 6, 1968, I awoke at my usual rising hour of 6:30 and turned on my bedside radio. It had happened again. Robert F. Kennedy had been cut down by Sirhan Sirhan in a Los Angeles hotel. I was swept with disbelief; just a few weeks before I had sat opposite him at a small luncheon and watched his fascinating eyes, which came with invisible shades that he pulled down whenever the conversation did not really interest him. But oh, the intensity, when the shades snapped up!

Norman Cousins, who knew him well, called me at my home. The July 1968 issue of *McCall's* was already being bound at the plant. At a staggering price, he had arranged that a last-minute page be bound in just inside the cover in most of the copies. Mary Kersey Harvey, his assistant, and I joined Norman in his office.

"I want to write a definitive editorial on violence that will stir this country into *doing* something that will prevent this from ever happening again," said Norman. "Let's each of us do a draft and I'll incorporate our thoughts into one." I spent all day at the typewriter, knowing Norman would probably not use any but his own material. But I was wrong; he took great chunks of my own thinking.

The editorial, "What Women Can Do to End Violence in America," is a classic of irony today. "American women . . . are sick with the collective havoc of the mindless crowd, and the individual savagery of those whose discontent has festered into rash destruction. The bullet that killed Robert F. Kennedy has wounded us all." Ideas were offered. Gun control. Asking networks and movie producers to tone down violence in their productions. And Norman's favorite cause: the pursuit of world order. (More recently, he has gone philosopho-medical; his *Anatomy of an Illness* tells how he cured a serious illness with laughter and mental control.)

Another stone dropped in a dark well. Another rallying cry echoing in the wind tunnel of contemporary history. Another largely unheard plea for sanity.

In the fall of 1968, it looked as if *McCall's* was about to have still one more editorial upheaval. I went to Herb

Mayes, who was the president of the company under Norton Simon, and asked if I could be considered as the next editor. He patted me on the head and said that despite my many talents, as far as he was concerned no woman could ever edit a mass women's magazine. Couldn't hack it, he felt.

Kenny Rogers tells us that the difference between holding and folding is what life is all about. As someone who really doesn't enjoy drastic change, I've always had a secret time clock in me that makes me triumph over my inertia and move at the right moment. In a deliberate act of career coquetry, I called Helen Meyer of Dell Publishing, and she said she'd find a berth for me there. As I knew she would, she called John Carter for a reference, and as I knew he would, he reacted with his usual competitiveness. He called me for breakfast the following morning, and in three days I was out of my dead-end and into Downe Publishing, home of the *Journal*. And, in the Kennedy context, into my Rose period.

I haven't spoken to Rose Kennedy recently. Frankly, I haven't had the courage since I excerpted the Gloria Swanson book, our section centering on the movie star's affair with Joe Kennedy. (He even put her on the same boat with his wife and family when they went to Europe.) But over the years I had a delightful relationship with this great lady and matriarch. And we have had many remarkable conversations.

I remember one beautiful September day we spent at Hyannis Port in 1969, working on the Christmas story already mentioned. She always got paid for interviews, giving the money to The Joseph P. Kennedy Foundation. Horst Horst, the fashionable photographer, was with me to take pictures, and I served as fashion consultant, makeup expert, and general factotum. As I helped her get dressed, I remarked that she still had the figure of a twenty-five-year-old.

"Most people say eighteen!" she responded with a twinkle. Four things about Rose Kennedy always impressed me: her strength, her absorptive and disciplined mind, her indomitable faith, and her vanity. We tried on several outfits, finally settling on a rose-colored Dior dress from the previous year's Paris collection, and a snappy Courrèges pantsuit, in which she looked like a little doll. I said so, and I meant it.

Several weeks later, she called me on the phone as she often did. In that unmistakable raspy Boston twang, she said, "Mrs. Hershey, you are always so interested in what I wear and how I look. I wonder if I could ask your advice. They're doing a memorial program for Bobby, and they want me to be on it. Is it all right to wear a pantsuit?"

"No," I said firmly. "I don't think so."

She sounded disappointed, like a little girl.

"But you thought I looked so nice in it. I intended to wear it down by the boats and all that," she added lamely.

"Wear the rose dress," I said. "You look lovely in it, and I think people will feel it is more appropriate."

And she did.

I had a few more sessions with Rose Kennedy, once as she took me and a few other people around the JFK birthplace at 83 Beals Street in Brookline, Massachusetts. Another time I visited her in the Central Park South apartment the family kept, trying to persuade her to get the whole family together for a portrait. But the interview I remember best, because it was so affecting, was the visit I had with her on a winter day in 1972 at Palm Beach, Florida. I had arranged to do a by-lined story with her to be called "How Rose Keeps Growing," and once more we handed over a sizable check for The Joseph P. Kennedy Foundation.

A taxi took me to the Kennedy home on North Ocean Boulevard, a mansion designed by the late Addison Mizner, one of the great Palm Beach architects. The chauffeur-caretaker, a Mr. Ryan, met me. (Later, I learned that his wife had taken an overdose of pills the week before and died.) He led me through the deserted, almost dingy house into a small, damp study. The only things lighting up the shabbiness of the room were the pictures on the walls, and the framed photos which spilled out everywhere. Next door was the dining room, with a huge dining table in the center. At one end, a single place mat, flanked by five medicine bottles. The scene spoke volumes.

Mrs. Kennedy came in, wearing the same Courrèges suit and neat little Gucci moccasins. We discussed the story; she no longer wanted to concentrate on motherhood.

"It's all out of date now," she said. "With population control and everything. So we can talk about anything."

This time I taped it all, except when she asked me to turn it off so that I could review the speech she was delivering that night for an Albert Einstein College of Medicine banquet. I urged her to refer to the country not as Palestine, but as Israel.

Then we walked about for a few minutes. On the piano were color miniatures of the Aaron Shikler portraits of JFK and Jackie that hang in the White House.

"I don't like them, do you?" she said.

. I mumbled something.

"They were a Christmas gift from Jackie. Personally, I wouldn't say they were my taste."

There was a photo of Rose as a young woman being presented at the Court of St. James's. She looked exquisite, and we paused to gaze at it. It stood in front of a mirror, and suddenly, in an unforgettable tableau, I caught a view of her in the mirror, over the picture frame.

"You really don't look that much different," I said. "Older, yes. But not that much different." The Rose in the mirror smiled enchantingly.

We took snapshots of each other on my small camera. (Stanley Tretick would take top-quality ones later.) Rose frankly discussed her retarded daughter, Rosemary, whom she saw at Christmas. I asked her what she would wear for the party that night, and she answered, "A pink Givenchy. Although if Givenchy doesn't give me a better discount, I'm going to say I buy all my clothes at Jordan Marsh!"

It was an intimate, rewarding visit, which I remember with loving feelings. I still have some notes I organized when I got back to the typewriter, and I think they are better than the story that appeared. I speak of the sadness, and the ultimate tragedy of knowing that there is no real privilege, that everyone faces the plight of being left old and alone. I recognize that she is a hedonist, with a young woman's ego about both her body and her mind, and that she is surviving with grace, outliving her strong husband and some of her strongest children. I talk of my admiration, not because she was the mother of John and Bobby and was hit by so many of history's blows, but because she is a woman who knows the score, and has made her peace with it in a woman's way.

Today I think she may even have forgiven me for running the Gloria Swanson book.

Jackie. She was another kind of original. Jacqueline Bouvier. I first heard about her from Perle Mesta, who met her in 1953 at Perle's home in London during the coronation of Queen Elizabeth. Jackie was on assignment as an inquiring camera girl for the now defunct *Times Herald* in Washington, and Perle invited her to a ball she was giving at Londonderry House for President Eisenhower's official representatives to the coronation. Jackie wrote it up as "Mesta's Fiesta," and when she went home, she was met at the airport, Perle recalled, by Jack Kennedy. Their engagement was announced shortly afterward.

When she was Jacqueline Kennedy, First Lady, I was simply one of those in the audience, admiring her taste, her grace, and her beauty. (She was one of those people who, as many models do, photograph even better than they look in person.) Mostly, I wondered how she would fare in the rough-and-tumble of Kennedy family activities. Or even more important, how she would take the Kennedy good ole boy philosophy of the freewheeling private life. To them, sex was a pastime, a sport like touch football, and a family code.

I quote Theodore B. White, the historian to whom Jackie chose to give her famous *Camelot* interview. In his own book, he writes about himself in the third person and says:

"He knew that Kennedy loved his wife—but that Kennedy, the politician, exuded that musk odor of power that acts as an aphrodisiac to many women. White was reasonably sure that only three Presidential candidates he had ever met had denied themselves the pleasures invited by that aphrodisiac—Harry Truman, George Romney and Jimmy Carter. [Perle had said practically the same thing.] He was reasonably sure that all the others he had met had, at one time or another, on the campaign trail, accepted casual partners."

Nor was it just on the campaign trail. Even after he was elected President, the press and other insiders traded each new story with lip-smacking relish, and some of us wondered why the Secret Service, if nobody else, did not get nervous.

The stories were rampant. There was one I tried to track

down: an earlier marriage with a Palm Beach socialite that
was supposed to be on the records somewhere before it was
annulled. If it had been on the records, it was forever
erased.

In New York, the talk centered on the secret over-the-
rooftops pathway from the Hotel Carlyle to the apartment
of Florence Pritchett Smith (wife of the U.S. Ambassador to
Cuba), who at first was JFK's partner, and then a kind of
talent scout. In Washington, they mulled over the position
of Angie Dickinson, who was at the Inaugural alone, and
who in a later interview with the *Journal* said that she did
not have an affair with JFK. (Except that when I once
visited her in Hollywood, there was a Secret Service man
hovering around.) Everywhere, they talked about the famous Marilyn Monroe appearance at JFK's Madison
Square Garden birthday party. (Jacqueline Susann personally assured me that the flirtation was consummated later in
the evening.) All of this was part of the JFK legend while he
was alive, including the rumor that old Joe paid Jackie a
million dollars not to leave him. Middle-class America did
not give it all much credence, which is probably just as well.
And after his death, the stories became less relevant, and
Jackie was left with the burden of the legend, and the right
to create her own rumors.

About a year into her widowhood, I had my first of many
encounters with that exuberant macho actor Anthony
Quinn. I will never forget our first lunch, in which he
moved from absolute hostility into a fascinating dissertation
on me, women, magazines, and Mrs. Kennedy, who he felt
was wasting her life. It ended with an ambitious plan to
have him edit a whole issue of *McCall's* in partnership with
Jackie Kennedy, provided I could set up a date for him to
discuss it with her. Once in a while, I pull rabbits out of
hats, and I actually did arrange this meeting. I know they

met in her apartment, and I know they went jogging later in Central Park, where they were spotted by *Women's Wear*. She declined the assignment. Where else it all went, I do not know.

When I moved to the *Journal,* Tony came up to the offices on the first day to bring me some flowers, and he did his Zorba the Greek dance up and down the aisles, which impressed my new associates no end. Later, he insisted that Jackie was smitten by Onassis only because Quinn had introduced her to his Zorba character. And it all ended up in still another article. Because as it worked out, Tony starred as Onassis in the movie *The Greek Tycoon,* which came out the summer of 1978. (He knew Aristotle Onassis; as he tells it, Onassis told him that if anyone were to play him in a film, he would like it to be Tony.)

It gets more complicated. When Mrs. Onassis heard that Tony was about to appear in a film about her late husband, she had her former secretary and now a Doubleday editor, Nancy Tuckerman, call him and tell him that she'd prefer it if he did not accept the part. ("She didn't call Robert Redford and tell him not to appear in *The Candidate,*" huffed Tony's practical wife.)

As Tony was making this painful decision, he happened to be lunching with his wife and Simone Signoret in a restaurant in St. Paul-de-Vence, near Cannes. "Here's your dearest friend," said his wife. In walked Jackie Onassis— and *cut him dead.* P.S. He took the part; it was a pretty dreadful movie, and I knocked that one off as one of my low-rated blind date arrangements.

Another time, I was busy working with Jackie's sister Lee Radziwill on her memoirs, tentatively titled *Opening Chapters.* She was anxious to meet publishers, so she agreed that we could give her a party at the Four Seasons, provided we turned out all the biggest publishers in town. They came; so did Norman Mailer and Truman Capote. And toward the end, in swept Jackie and stole the show. Phyllis Levy, my great book editor who rounded up all the publishers, chuckled at the way these sophisticated gents pushed each other aside just to get close to this fabulous lady. I don't know how Lee felt, but later she and Jackie collaborated on a memoir of their childhood, *One Special Summer,* which did get published and did not do well.

Eventually, Jackie went into publishing herself, first at Viking and then at Doubleday, where she has been recently promoted to editor. At Viking, she came back into my ken again as she worked on *Journal of the Century,* a handsome volume tracing the whole history of the *Journal,* and containing some of the best literary and graphic examples of every period. So, in a way, she *did* become a women's magazine editor.

I admire Jackie Bouvier Kennedy Onassis today. She is growing older with strength and grace; she is her own woman; and she has managed to survive the indignity of having Jacqueline Bisset and Jackie Smith play her on the screen, both of which impersonations I trust she found more amusing than disturbing. I hope she marries again, I hope he's rich, and I hope nobody will be cast for *his* role in the movie version until we're all gone.

Ted Kennedy. I guess it's hard to leave him out, although history has seemed to make an effort of doing so. He is a brilliant legislator, a tremendously driven man with a commitment that often has dazzled me. But he has always poured on torrents of that musk Teddy White refers to, and the stories about him outdo even the ones about JFK. Joan I got to know early on, and she was one of those people who you knew was going to end up getting hurt. She had a bad habit of confiding in sympathetic interviewers, and my male

51

executive editor, while never revealing her secrets, certainly could have written a book if he'd wanted to.

About Chappaquiddick, which seems to be the great unsolved legend of our time, I have only theories. We assigned stories by everyone, including F. Lee Bailey. We went up there ourselves and looked at the bridge. We approached Mary Jo Kopechne's family. The wonder of Chappaquiddick is that nobody who might know has ever broken the pact of silence. (Ever-voracious Maxine Cheshire once told me that it was her theory that there was still another date back at the motel on the mainland, but I discount that.) My own feeling? I think the drowned girl was sleeping in the back seat, that Teddy was heading for the beach with another of the young women, and the whole thing was too protectively handled. And if the real, authoritative story *is* ever told, it will be told by Esther Newberg, a young woman at the party, who is now a literary agent, and who is saving her own book until such time as she deems advisable.

Kennedys. The stories go on and on. Caroline at three, Caroline at sixteen, John John at twenty-one, Caroline at twenty-four. Jackie at fifty. The birthdays all merge and meld, as do the stories. New people appear on the scene, but at parties all over the world I am still asked over and over again for anecdotes about them. And I still pick up interesting tidbits. Example: In the fall of 1981, Joan Kennedy went to Rosh Hashanah services at the Swampscott synagogue with her Jewish psychologist boyfriend. A woman I met at a medical banquet happened to be sitting behind Joan at the services. (I do well at medical banquets. More recently, a doctor next to me gave me all the details of Dolly Parton's "tummy tucks," which she quietly had done in a New York hospital.)

There is only one other legend about which I am asked almost as often as I am about Kennedys.

Did Eisenhower really have an affair with his wartime driver, Kay Summersby?

I reach far back for part of the answer. When I was working at the *New York Herald Tribune* in my salad days, the owner, Helen Rogers Reid (a good model for Mrs. Pynchon on the now-defunct *Lou Grant Show*), got together with her man-in-charge, Bill Robinson, Clare Boothe Luce, Joe Alsop, and others to draft General Eisenhower to run on the Republican ticket for President, even though he had been more or less of a Democrat. There were some problems. Some way had to be found to get him some financial security. Mamie was possibly too fragile. And there was Kay Summersby. The first hurdle was surmounted by a book, created in cooperation with Ken McCormick of Doubleday, and utilizing a law that had just been passed in Congress that allowed an amateur to take capital gains on a project already in work. (The book, *Crusade in Europe*, largely ghosted by Joe Barnes, netted Eisenhower $600,000.) Mamie was found to be less of a problem than expected: Her drinking was not the sole cause of her seeming shaky on occasions; there was also a physiological balance problem. And Kay Summersby, I was told, was bought off and given a job at Bergdorf Goodman, where she worked for years.

But my last authority, once more, was Perle Mesta. She was an old friend of Mamie's. They both lived at the old Wardman Park Hotel in Washington—now the Sheraton Park—and she had been very close to Mamie ever since Ike had come to Washington as a colonel. Perle and I went down to visit Mamie in Gettysburg in 1964, to do a story on the twentieth anniversary of D-Day. It was a marvelous day. We wandered around and looked at Ike's barbecue, went over old memorabilia, and sat on the round sofa copied from those in the lobby of the Brown Palace Hotel in

Denver. (I had to help Mamie down even the smallest of steps: Her balance was that bad.)

On the way home in the limo, I put it to Perle straight. "Did Ike ever really want to leave Mamie and marry Kay Summersby?"

"He sure did," said Perle. "His naval aide's wife, Ruth Butcher, was living with Mamie at the hotel at that time, and she told Mamie one night her husband had just asked her for a divorce to marry a woman he had met overseas. And Mrs. Butcher said of course she was going to give him the divorce."

"Ruth was foolish," Perle told me she clearly remembered Mamie saying. "Ike also asked me for a divorce and I flatly refused. You know these things blow over and men move on to other things. I intend to be beside him when he comes home."

We printed "Past Forgetting: My Love Affair with Dwight D. Eisenhower" in the December 1976 issue of the *Journal*. (Kay Summersby Morgan died in 1975, of cancer of the liver.) The book was supposedly written by her before her death, but in truth most of the writing was done by Barbara Wyden, ex-wife of ex-*Journal* editor Peter Wyden. The book portrayed a deep, romantic love affair, which technically never did get down to complete sex, although there certainly seemed to be a lot of cuddling and kissing and some talk about a future child. The problem was, it seems, that Eisenhower's sex drives had been dimmed by his past life, although frankly I hated the way the news stories kept talking about his "impotence." (I thought Kay . . . or Barbara . . . protested too much.) At any rate, he abruptly left her and returned home to Mamie and the presidency of Columbia University, and eventually the White House. Proving that Mamie was right.

The mail on this story was very heavy, most of it critical.

The chief beef seemed to be the inclusion of the book in a Christmas issue, followed by the obvious objection to having it printed while Mamie was still alive. I would have preferred that not to have happened myself, but Simon & Schuster chose the book publication date, and I had no choice. There was some favorable mail, too. Many readers felt that it provided new human dimensions to Eisenhower.

About a year or so afterward, before Mamie went into her final illness, I wrote her a letter in longhand. I did not mention the book. But I recalled the day we spent in Gettysburg, Perle and I, and the beautiful evening in which Mamie had appeared on our *Journal* "Women of the Year" television show with Rosalind Russell at Kennedy Center. I told her how much the nation admired her, and I apologized for any hurt I or other members of the press had brought to her. I had no ulterior motive, and very few people know I wrote the letter. But I wanted to do it.

I never heard directly from Mamie. But Julie Eisenhower called me one day and said Mrs. Eisenhower had told her she had received a very moving letter from me.

That, too, was a moment past forgetting.

THREE

Best-Seller Fever

Magazines have always used books and authors to fortify their content. Reciprocally, book publishers and writers regard magazines as friendly providers of added exposure, prestige, and income. *Ladies' Home Journal,* for example, has consistently been a showcase for literary talents: in the old days, for such as Thomas Hardy, Edith Wharton, Rudyard Kipling, and in modern times, James Michener, Norman Mailer, Daphne du Maurier.

Today, with about 40,000 new book titles out there every year, there is a wealth of works from which to winnow winners. Most books fall by the wayside as wrong for the targeted audience, or not practical for the space crunch of a magazine. But many make it. And the really hot ones are sought with bloodthirsty competitiveness by editors who plot their blitzkrieg purchasing campaigns as if their lives depended on wrestling a property from the opposition.

The threats of rising costs and shrinking profits now throw dark shadows over the shared worlds of books and magazines. Where once there were free-standing businesses run by professional individualists, now there are complex corporations, many of them diversified conglomerates. The shots are being increasingly called by young financial zingers whose only required reading is the *Wall Street Journal* and computer printouts. Toting their calculators and mouthing initials, these MBAs couldn't tell a metaphor from a macaroon. But they are very big in DCFROI, which means Discounted Cash Flow Return on Investment, and also Don't Court Failure with Rebels, Originals, or Intellectuals. Especially in tough times.

Magazine editors, too, find themselves increasingly crouching between the balance sheets, coping with fewer pages, smaller budgets, and more kibitzing from the executive suite. But editing always has been far, far more than bottom-line strategy. Editing is intuition and heart. Editing is knowing what readers want before *they* know, and before the researchers have the chance to survey. Editing is understanding human beings, not just demographics. Editing is falling in love with ideas, and respecting the craft of verbal and graphic artists. Editing is orchestrating by instinct. No matter how rough times are, the editors who will make it for the financial projections are the ones who are listening to their own inner voices, who believe in the courage of creativity, not the omnipotence of numbers. (If their magazines stay in business, I add bitterly.)

The cold truth is that the purchase of books is not a mass audience industry in the United States. Despite the proliferation of big bookstores—the two retail chains which own Dalton's and Waldenbooks expect to have 2,500 stores by 1985—a best-selling hardcover book can make the best-seller list with a sale of a hundred thousand copies or less; a paperback, with under half a million.

This is small potatoes when compared to the multimillion audiences of the big magazines, and even slighter spuds against the huge audiences of such talk shows as Phil Donahue, Johnny Carson, and Merv Griffin, where an author's appearance can plump up sales by healthy percentage points.

It also helps when the author does a dog-and-pony tour, touching base with local TV and cable shows, and signing books in stores.

A cover line on a magazine such as the *Ladies' Home Journal* also provides a push, especially among women. And the strength of line, if it's a flashy one, helps to sell magazines, even if what's inside is only a teasing taste. There are some agents and publishers who won't touch magazine condensations, or even excerpts, feeling that it steals the show, but most love the exposure. I do think that our *Journal* two-part condensation cut into sales of Betty Ford's inspiring autobiography, *The Times of My Life.* We bought the rights for $125,000 after a long and hard-fought auction, and really worked at making it look and read well, so that readers got, for $1.25 a copy, a bargain in reading which would have cost $10.95 at the bookstore. I once admitted to Betty Ford that I thought the *Journal* was responsible for keeping her off the best-seller lists, but she didn't seem bothered. (We also co-hosted a big, lavish party for her at the Waldorf, where all the top-drawer celebrities were more interested in her recent face-lift than in her book.)

Books in magazines are usually bought "first serial," which means they are used before the publishing date. And many of them are bought long before the reviews, at something called a multiple submission book auction.

Let's say that Elizabeth Taylor is going to write her autobiography, which she's been threatening to do at some point. Magazines know this is surefire, so at the first rumor they start besieging her literary agent. If the agent decides that a pre-emptive bid is in order, one magazine can block out the rest with an overwhelming figure, say a million dollars. But this kind of bidding is unlikely, so everyone waits for this E.T. to finish her book. When it is completed and sold to a publisher, an auction date is set. If before the auction an editor wants to

59

read the book, so she is not bidding on a pig in a poke, elaborate arrangements are set up for confidential readings, sometimes even with papers to be signed that legally bind the editor to keep things secret and not leak them immediately to columnists.

Next comes the big day: the poker game of the actual round-robin telephone auction. In their separate offices, a lot of chief editors who have a pretty good idea of what their competitors are thinking decide how much they are going to spend, based on the property and the timing. (Usually, the editor has the cover line written, too: "FINALLY! ELIZABETH TAYLOR TELLS HER OWN STORY! The secrets nobody ever knew about her marriages, her children, her illnesses, the hidden passion she has never revealed. . . .") The *Journal*, like a canny riverboat gambler, starts the round off with $50,000. At *Good Housekeeping* and *McCall's*, they raise the ante to $75,000. *Woman's Day* and *Family Circle*, each sensing the other's desire to get the book, both come in at $100,000. *Cosmopolitan* is out of it because the stakes are too high. *Reader's Digest* is complicated, because they usually make handsome deals directly with publishers for condensed book rights for their book club—and then shut out all other magazine sales. In this case, let's say they are not playing.

The agent comes back to the *Journal* and says that the ceiling is now $100,000. (I've always wondered why we all blindly trust the agents' quotes. I guess they are inhibited by the fact that most of us on magazines will check later and flush out any discrepancies.) The editor, by now, is playing with big bucks and seeks the approval of the publisher and company president, who usually can be persuaded if the buy is right. Now comes the tricky part. Should one raise by $5,000 or $10,000? Should it be in round numbers or in jagged ones . . . like $117,000.50? (At least twice, this technique worked.) Now the ribbon clerks, or the editors with stingy presidents, start dropping out. Everybody cancels late afternoon appointments to find out who won.

I guess some of the biggest thrills I remember in my editing career are those occasions when dark-haired, ever-slim, book and fiction editor Phyllis Levy stood in my doorway, flushed with excitement, interrupting whatever I was doing to shout: "We've got it! We've got it! So-and-so will be absolutely furious, they were so dying to have it. But *we've* got it!"

And we did get them, over and over again at the *Journal:* James Michener with *The Drifters, Hawaii, Centennial, The Covenant*. All excerpted, of course. It would take a hundred issues to serialize a full Michener novel. Erich Segal, Leon Uris, Daphne du Maurier, Chaim Potok, Anton Myrer, Irving Wallace, Norman Mailer, Avery Corman, Evan Hunter, Agatha Christie, and so many, many more authors of our time and their big books. .

Once in a while, of course, I did make a mistake. Like persuading myself to do business with that would-be author Spiro Theodore Agnew, the first Vice-President in United States history to resign under duress, and also the first Vice-President with the *chutzpah* to write a novel, a fact which I must say impressed me by its singularity.

His agent, Scott Meredith, one of the best, informed me that he had the same reaction when Agnew called him.

"I told him my politics were diametrically opposed to his," says Scott. "And Agnew said that was fine with him. Then I assured myself that he was actually doing the book himself."

Before I completely capitulated, I sent our keen, hard-to-fool Articles Editor Mary Fiore down to see Agnew in Maryland. She came home convinced that this was all on the up-and-up. So we negotiated with Scott Meredith for an early chapter of the book, eventually titled *The Canfield Decision,* plus a signed article by Agnew to be called "The Truth About My Novel," which we then scheduled for the May 1974 issue of the *Journal. The New York Times* caught wind of the negotiations and broke a big story on February 6. Although we had arranged to pay only $65,000 for the package, with an option to get more later, the *Times* headline was MAGAZINE IS SAID TO PAY $100,000 FOR AGNEW NOVEL. I was quoted as coyly saying, "We always like to encourage new writers," adding, "The book sounds like a whopping good suspense story, with a Washington background, which I always love."

I knew I was taking a chance. Agnew, after all, had pleaded nolo contendere to a charge of income tax evasion after being implicated in a kickback scheme. It was also in the middle of the anti-Vietnam movement, and Bob Bernstein of Random House had turned down the Agnew novel proposal as not suitable for their list. But as I said, I was intrigued by the uniqueness and newsworthiness of the book, and the sample I was given to read was quite professional.

But I never anticipated the force of the reaction. Telegrams and letters poured in criticizing us for buying the novel from such a discredited public official. My own friends and relatives were acerbic. I found myself saying that I never did a political test on any writer before we bought a book, and feeling uneasy because it sounded as if I were on his side. I did not ever meet Mr. Agnew, although we did talk by phone. Once, on another errand, I was with President Nixon in the Oval Office and I casually mentioned that we were going to run Agnew's novel. Nixon muttered something like "Mmmm." "Have you read it?" I asked mischievously. "I have not," he answered coldly. End of that conversation.

Going back now to the issue of May 1974, it is spooky to read Agnew's own outline of the book. He describes it as a novel about "a Vice-President who becomes a dupe of Iranian militants who want to cause an all-out confrontation between the U.S. and the Soviet Union. The militants mistakenly believe that Russia is planning to take over Afghanistan. Fearing that Iran will be the next country to be overrun by the Soviets, the militants plot the U.S.-Soviet facedown by heating up the Arab-Israeli conflict." My query: How did Spiro Agnew, who even then was representing American business interests in the Arab countries, get the jump on history?

The book came out some time later, made the best-seller lists for a couple of weeks, and according to Playboy Books, who published it, earned $122,176.12, on which I trust Mr. Agnew paid taxes. It was also reprinted abroad, in England, Taiwan, Japan, and, of course, Greece. For the record, the May 1974 issue of the *Journal* was not one of our best sellers. So I am not distressed by the fact that Mr. Agnew, now living near his good friend Frank Sinatra in Rancho Mirage, California, has not sent us any manuscripts lately.

Another questionable book, as I look back, came up while I was managing editor of the *Journal*. In the September 1972 issue, our top cover line was:

WHAT REALLY HAPPENED
CLIFFORD IRVING WRITES HIS OWN STORY OF THE HOWARD HUGHES HOAX

It was a story of greed, conspiracy, fraud, and gullibility. A second-rate writer, Clifford Irving, decided to exploit the hunger of publishers and the media for material on the reclusive, fascinating magnate and legend Howard Hughes, by an elaborate plot to write his "authorized autobiography" from completely invented taped interviews. He cooked up a scheme that convinced Al Leventhal at McGraw-Hill, a reputable and important publishing house, that he was acting in Howard Hughes' interest. He actually received checks up to $275,000 which were deposited in a Swiss bank by Irving's wife, Edith, posing as Helga R. Hughes. Even as his wife was doing this, Irving was having an affair with the Danish wife of a baron,

Nina Van Pallandt, an attractive woman who subsequently sang in nightclubs. The book's authenticity was swallowed whole by McGraw-Hill and Time, Inc., until finally the illusion collapsed. Howard Hughes came out of retirement at his Paradise Island retreat in the Bahamas to hold a telephone press conference on Mike Wallace's *Sixty Minutes* TV show. As he had previously told a *Time* bureau chief, he had never met anyone named Clifford Irving in his life. Eight Los Angeles newsmen on the show confirmed that the denial was being issued by the *real* Howard Hughes, and the jig was up. Both Clifford Irving and his wife served two years in jail, she doing her sentence first so one parent would be left to take care of the children. (Recently, the publishing world has forgiven Irving, and he has had two novels . . . up-front fiction . . . published.)

It still is an amazing tale and I must admit that at the time I was uncomfortable with its appearance in the *Journal*, although we made sure not to condone its sordid illegality. Again we received a great deal of unfavorable mail, but this one did sell copies, since Howard Hughes for a long time was one of those mystery people who attracted readers.

Among the reporters on the *Sixty Minutes* show attesting to the identity of Hughes on the Clifford Irving matter was one of my favorite people in Hollywood, Vernon Scott, who contributed many pieces to the *Journal* over the years and who now writes for *Good Housekeeping*. He is the source of many of my best Hughes anecdotes, and one appeared in a story he did for us in 1970, "The Liberation of Mrs. Howard Hughes." After thirteen years of marriage, Jean Peters Hughes was getting a divorce, and Vernon had tracked her down and even managed to get some details about a new man in her life. Suddenly, Vernon had the uncomfortable feeling he was being watched. Sure enough, before he turned his story in, Vernon was approached by a man he knew was in the Hughes organization and was offered $25,000 to give up the story. Vernon refused.

A few mornings later, a stranger rang his doorbell and offered to trade a brand-new Mercedes Benz 380 SE for Vernon's old Mustang. When pressed for details, the caller did admit he also wanted the rights to the Jean Peters story. A few hours later, Vernon's wife, Jane, called him from a diner where she was having lunch with their two children.

"You won't believe this," said Jane. "But a man sitting next to me has just offered to trade cars with me. He has a new Mercedes, and he wants ours for some crazy reason."

"Forget it," said Vernon. "I turned that offer down this morning." And we did run the story, without changing it.

Vernon is a great raconteur of Hughes anecdotes. One I always recall when I'm in an airport restroom is about Howard Hughes and his then girlfriend, actress Terry Moore. Terry had once told Vernon of a great plane ride they took together in his small one-prop private plane out to somewhere in the Grand Canyon area. When nature called, Howard Hughes decided to land his plane and use the facilities of a small airport hangar. He hopped out of the plane, ran several hundred yards to the building. In a few minutes he ran back, uncomfortable and furious.

"Let me have a dime," he shouted at Terry. "They've only got one stall and it's a pay booth. And I'll be damned if I'll crawl under the door." She fortunately had a dime.

Not only did he never pay her back, but according to Terry he sent out a note banning pay toilets at all TWA terminals, a rule unfortunately now abandoned. I hope that when Warren Beatty does his upcoming film on Hughes *(Beds?)*, he will go back to some of Sheilah Graham's H.H. memories. Sheilah, who followed Zelda in the love life of F. Scott Fitzgerald, was a Hollywood columnist, and she knew Hughes well. One night, he got her out of bed with a 102-degree fever to give her a "scoop." The scoop turned out to be merely a derogatory story about director Stanley Donen, then the current partner of Elizabeth Taylor. Mr. Hughes, too, was one of the torch carriers for Elizabeth Taylor, but she thought he was just a dirty old man. Speaking of dirty old men, I once had lunch in Paris with Sheilah and author Henry Miller, whose books were once banned for their explicit sexuality. Except that in person Miller wasn't dirty. He was mellow and darling.

Authors, authors, I've known so many of them, and only a few reflect the style and flavor of their work.

Like Jacqueline Susann, who could have been one of her own characters. She was unexpurgated, uninhibited, and unrelenting, but I loved her.

Many of the critics had it in for Jackie, resenting not so much the way she wrote, but the amount of money she made at it. As her friend Rex Reed said in a beautiful memorial he did for me at the *Journal,* "Her books were better than most people credited them with being. They had warmth, humor, wit, sharply-defined characters, startling plot twists, hypnotic story lines, and enough thinly disguised public figures to keep cocktail parties guessing and every movie star in Hollywood fighting to get into the movie versions."

Along with my husband and my daughter, then at college, I was lucky enough to become part of the circle of Jackie's and Irving's friends. It was a circle with a large circumference, but a warm one. To be a friend of the Mansfields, as Barbara Walters, Anna Sosenko, Helen Gurley Brown and her husband David, Doris Day, Oscar Dystel, Esther Margolis, and others knew, was not a casual matter. She took friendship seriously. Once she drove my daughter Jane down to the University of Pennsylvania—in a limo, natch—and dazzled her by a literary discussion of Zola, whose novels had, she said, influenced her own. She brought Joseph, her second poodle, up to our house to visit Brillo, the poodle she had given me. She came to our parties with Irving and we went to their big bashes, with their wall-to-wall celebrity guests. Irving and

Jackie, wearing one of her many Puccis, invited Sol and me out to dinner at Le Madrigal when I became editor-in-chief, and volunteered to write anything I wanted. Originally, we thought she might do an article to be called "Jackie O. by Jackie S," and I called her at the Beverly Hills Hotel to suggest it. But the first draft was pretty bad. "Let me write it as fiction," she said, and I agreed.

And so *Dolores* was born, later sketched out over lunch at the Four Seasons. We waffled about it in the publicity, for legal reasons, but it was designed as a novella, a *roman à clef* obviously based on Jacqueline Onassis, although the heroine was Dolores Cortez, widowed when her husband, Jimmy Ryan, President of the United States, is struck down in mid-term by a heart attack. Dolores marries an aging French tycoon, who leaves her on their wedding night for a famous ballerina. Jackie Susann charged the magazine only $20,000 for the manuscript, which she never really meant to publish as a book, although Irving did bring it out in book form after her death. The February 1974 issue of the *Journal,* in which it ran, was our all-time best seller at the newsstands.

And all the time, she kept those terrible personal secrets to herself. Early in their marriage, she and Irving had a son, Guy. He had very early shown the worst symptoms of autistic behavior and had to be institutionalized for the rest of his life. I always suspected that it was this tragedy that riveted Jackie and Irving together, and that their shared interest in her books was almost as if the books themselves had become substitute offspring. At any rate, their devotion was very real, and unusual in the show-biz world in which they moved. In 1962, she discovered a lump in her breast, which turned out to be malignant. She had a mastectomy, which she also never told anybody about. For ten years she lived a normal life, but then the cancer moved on to her lungs and her bronchi. But she went on gallantly, allowing nobody, not even her intimates, to share her pain and suffering. *Valley of the Dolls* stayed on the top of the best-seller lists for 65 weeks, while Jackie kept busy writing *Once Is Not Enough*. She was a frequent guest on all the big talk shows, and became even more of a celebrity as she feuded with Truman Capote (he referred to her as "a truck driver in drag") and critic John Simon. At the end, she was in a coma for seven weeks, opening her eyes only long enough to say to Irving, "Hey doll, let's get the hell outa here." At her funeral, the same hundreds who came to her parties came to pay honor and to mourn, and the tears were real. As she had requested, Irving put her ashes in a copper volume which he kept on a bookshelf. He once told me it had an eerie, chaperone-across-the-Styx effect on him whenever he brought a woman up to the apartment. The ashes are now elsewhere.

Of course, I used to have quite a different type of experience with Truman Capote, who also went out of his way to offer guidance and support when I became editor-in-chief. We would lunch at Le Pavillon, the old Henri Soule restaurant on Fifty-seventh Street located where the Women's Bank now stands. Truman's dishing over the haute cuisine dishes was an adventure in style. That unforgettable and often imitated nasal intonation, his delight in shocking you with horrific details about people in high places, his brilliant evaluation of people and situations, all were well worth the price of lunch, which was astronomic. How I remember him telling me the story of how he had received an injection in his buttock from Dr. Max Jacobson, the "Dr. Feelgood" who gave injections to the Kennedys and other celebrities. It was an injection in paraffin, and it wasn't just vitamins. By the time Truman got to Switzerland, he said, he had to enter a sanitorium and be detoxified from a good dose of amphetamine, or "speed." Poor Truman. Between booze and drugs, he lay waste his powers and hindered one of the greatest writing talents of his time.

He was having a writing block even then. *In Cold Blood* had

taken five years, and after its final revision, he gave that famous black and white ball for "five hundred people I liked." I
visited him in his apartment high above the East River to
persuade him to write a short story for us. What a contrast
between the plump, balding man in his forties and that photograph in his apartment that also appears on the dust jacket of
Other Voices, Other Rooms—an outrageous, sensuous boy, a sort
of male Brooke Shields, peering under his blond bangs at a
world he was about to conquer.

He did the piece for us, not exactly a short story, but a
reminiscence called "The White Rose," about an early meeting with the French novelist Colette, who gave him a crystal
Baccarat paperweight with a white rose engraved in its heart,
and who told him she had been warned about Truman:
"Don't be fooled—he looks like a ten-year-old angel. But he's
ageless, and he has a very wicked mind." Remembering this, I
decided to court him again for my first issue as editor-in-chief,
and my right-hand, Dick Kaplan, and I drove out to have
lunch with him on Long Island and to make a devilish
proposition.

"Truman," I said, "we have something that will be so easy
for you to write, and such fun, that you can't say no. It's a
chance to convert your matchless art of gossip into something
else."

The assignment we outlined was called "Blind Items," in
which Truman would tell some of his best stories about people
without identifying them. It became the lead piece in my first
issue, January 1974. He prefaced the five vignettes by explaining that blind items originated in the early nineteenth-century
guttersnipe press as a kind of blackmail—that is, to induce the
anonymous though identifiable subjects to pay off the writer
to prevent him from repeating his mischievous, occasionally
criminal allegations. Our lawyers, who were agitated at the
whole idea, finally cleared the articles, I suspect because they

didn't recognize the people the articles were about. One story concerned an American diplomat and a young British beauty who had a fling at the end of World War II, but separated because he was married and had a career. Years and years later, after they were both married and widowed, they were married and his accountant reminded him that he had been paying her $20,000 a year all these years. I was told that Averell Harriman and his wife, Pamela, were furious at Truman. Another was a thinly veiled anecdote about what seemed to be still another of President Kennedy's amours.

Truman had agreed to give us two installments of these stories. When the second batch came in, I realized we could not handle them. This time the stories were so cruel, so damaging, so truly wicked, that I chose to send Truman his check and forget the whole thing. One, I remember, was about a socialite whom he inferred was not only guilty of adultery and bigamy, but also of murdering her husband under the pretense she had thought he was a prowler. I was uncertain about the identity of other personalities in the group, so Truman sent me a shameless identifying code, which I fortunately destroyed, but vividly recall.

Though we did not use the material, Truman found use for it. He adapted the material and converted it into a novel he was supposed to have been working on: *Answered Prayers*. (He just recently stated he's now going to finish this oft-abandoned project.) *Esquire* printed whatever he wrote as fast as he could turn it out, and this time the reaction set in. The people to whom he so transparently alluded, and their friends, thought it unconscionable. *Esquire* sold out. Many people felt Truman did, too. Especially when the socialite he verbally crucified took her own life, causing a wave of real anger in circles that knew the facts. Most recently, Truman's been meddling again, pathetically getting headlines because he felt he could change the von Bulow verdict by saying that Sunny von

Bulow was not given insulin by her convicted husband, but did it herself. It seems they had this delicious conversation about drug kicks, and she told Truman that it would be simple to shoot himself up because she did. Sick.

I guess lots of us have mixed emotions about Truman Capote. His unique and special talent, his feisty compassion for underdogs, his social butterfly vivacity, are all hard to resist. He never made any pretense about his sexual preference, even before homosexuality was fashionable. In one of our issues, he did a profile on Elizabeth Taylor and included a horrifying anecdote about their mutual friend, Montgomery Clift. Truman and he had lunched together at Le Pavillon, and "dear, dear Monty" had stopped in the men's room, where "he must have taken something," because they went on to Gucci's and Monty picked up two dozen expensive sweaters and threw them into the rainy street and started kicking them around. One of the Gucci salespeople asked Truman coolly, "To whom do we charge these?"

"My face is my charge card," Monty informed the Gucci staff. Truman told the tale with relish.

I hope someday there will be a definitive biography of Truman Capote, half as good as he could have done it in his prime. Meanwhile, he has surfaced again in the *Journal*. A story in the 1982 Christmas issue proves that the talent is still with him, and that his ear for human anguish remains astonishingly acute.

Norman Mailer is another nonconformist who always seems bent on being a tourist attraction as well as a literary titan. Because I was fortunate enough to have seen him more or less sober, he has always appeared to me to be a kind of rough-hewn talking teddy bear. One of the great conversations I had with him was in 1980, after the *Journal* bought *Of Women and Their Elegance*, a book I had avoided auction-bidding on by giving him a lot of money before it was written. It turned out to be, not a book about elegant women, but a self-styled "false memoir," in which Mailer pretended to be Marilyn Monroe writing her autobiography, accompanied by photographs taken by Milton Greene. In an effort to amplify the property, I offered $1,000 for a long luncheon interview. He came to lunch, declined the payment, and I think the notes of the interview are better than the book.

Once more he admitted he never met Marilyn; the closest he'd been was when he sat behind her at the Actors Studio. But he did feel an identity with her. She, too, had come out of nowhere and achieved notoriety. "I also remember this feeling of being projected into celebrity," said NM. "It's a bizarre feeling, like running a fever."

He repeated what he had expressed in *Prisoner of Sex*, about why men fear women.

"Women are part of those endless boxes within boxes which make up the true universe, while men are really on the outside knocking on the doors."

We talked about Brooklyn . . . "the whole Eastern seaboard encapsulated in one borough." . . . Jackie Onassis: "It would take a Proust to get inside her mind" . . . growing older: "You never feel older; it just takes you longer to get out of the chair."

It was a long lunch, but it flew on wings of provocative ideas. At sixty he still spills out that mixture of garrulous wisdom and balderdash that is his signature. He had made his mistakes—six marriages, including a messy incident in which he stabbed his second wife. He has mistakenly sponsored a murderer, Jack Henry Abbott, and refused to back down on his actions. He has been unkind to the women's movement. But since his literary debut in *The Naked and the Dead*, his powers have broadened and diversified rather than diminished. I am still a devotee of Mailer's dense, incisive prose, and willing to forgive his publicity stunts. I also hear he's nice to all those children he's collected in his string of marriages. I look forward to reading his newest, *Ancient Evenings,* part one of a trilogy.

Authors, authors. Unlike actors, their gifts often are not obvious. At *McCall's* I worked with a fast-talking, sometimes sharp-tongued promotion writer, another *gemütlich* Brooklyn boy. (He had also been a camper at my father's camp.) One day he said to me, "You know, I write, too." I nodded, approvingly, and probably with some condescension. Limericks, no doubt.

"Would you like to read the proofs of my new novel over the weekend?" That was something else again, and before I could say no, I was handed several pounds of paper.

I started to read the book on the train to Riverdale and almost missed my station. I spent the entire weekend dropping those galley proofs all over the house until my husband asked what had me so terribly involved.

"There's a man in my office who is an absolute blooming genius!" I said, making him listen to a few of the most dazzling paragraphs.

The book was *Catch-22* and the author was Joseph Heller. Joe came up to the house once or twice with his family (whom he later left) and I, like everybody else in the office, watched with pride and amazement as he became the author of the decade. I was one of those who reacted immediately to *Catch-22* as one of the classic novels of our time, and I don't think he ever matched it in his later career. I asked him once how he had written that memorable scene when Yossarian spills paper all over the floor of the plane. Joe, who also had been a navigator, shrugged and said: "Yeah, I think I remember one sheet dropping on the floor."

He later wrote *Something Happened,* which was supposedly inspired by life at *McCall's.* Joe and I had often discussed our mutual neurosis: a fear that when an executive's door is closed, he's in there doing something or saying something that is going to make you unhappy.

Sure enough, the opening sentences in *Something Happened* are:

> I get the willies when I see closed doors. Even at work where I am doing so well now, the sight of a closed door is sometimes horrible enough to make me dread that something horrible is going on behind it, something that will affect me adversely . . .

Joe Heller sent me an autographed copy of the book, with the inscription:

> Believe it or not I still get the willies when I see closed doors, but only the closed doors of book reviewers.

I always wondered about those sexual encounters in stairwells and the orgiastic parties he described as happening in the office. I guess they kept doors shut: I never saw anything steamy like that going on.

In December 1981, Heller was stricken with Guillain-Barré syndrome, a frightening neurological illness that can paralyze the entire body, and which can be life-threatening. Joe put up possibly the most vigorous fight of his life, survived a long hospital siege in intensive care and went on for rehabilitation to the Rusk Clinic. He is now at home making remarkable progress, driving a car and working on a new novel, which could be his best.

James Michener, whom I've also had a pleasant friendship with over the years, is another man whose deep talents are not immediately apparent. His mien is gentle; he looks like a college professor. His books are total immersion experiences in subjects he selects with precision timeliness: *Hawaii, The*

Source, Centennial, The Covenant. When we ran *Centennial* in the magazine, I had the treat of traveling with Michener on a private plane excursion to Denver, where we toured the Colorado oil country and he signed books on buses and beside oil wells. Now that he's conquered space and is taking on Texas, I recommend that Michener do a saga on women's magazines. I'd be pleased to help with research. Suggested title: *The Womb.*

Self-help, fulfillment, and improvement books are always big in women's magazines. Diet plans are surefire, although I had a personal rule about excluding any diet that was not nutritionally sound, or depended on gimmicks or drugs. We turned down the *Beverly Hills Diet* book, but I must admit that I let the Scarsdale diet get by me. I first glimpsed it on a mimeographed piece of paper brought into the office by a staffer whose mother was a patient of Dr. Tarnower, and I should have pounced then. Doctors, despite some signs of popular skepticism about their godlike qualities, are still not a hindrance to the effectiveness of a story. On the other hand, readers also gobble up the exposés which show, with documentation, that doctors are sometimes alcoholic, sometimes addicted to drugs, and sometimes make mistakes. The feet-of-clay syndrome, once more.

But because women's magazines are read by so many, and relied on as a kind of personal medical consultant, editors should have an informed responsibility. A certain number of stories should be run, without sensationalizing, about the subject of breast cancer. About the dangers of smoking, even though the cigarette companies are major advertisers. About medical breakthroughs in every field affecting women, with a tilt toward checking new "cures" before offering false hopes.

"Agony" books and excerpts are something else. The *Journal* was the magazine that ran the first full report of the Karen Quinlan case, in which a young woman's parents "pulled the plug" on their comatose daughter, who then went on to live in sleep for many years. Phyllis Battelle's account of this human and ethically historic drama was so sensitive, so moving, that Doubleday chose to turn it into a book. On the other hand, I believe that horror and blood and bizarre situations should not be exploited only for their morbid "There but for the grace of God go I" fascination. We are stimulated by the violence and drama of a road accident, but unless we can help, we should drive on—perhaps at lowered speed. In a magazine, this kind of overemphasized grimness has always seemed to be a cheap way to attract readers.

While I was editing, our regular psychiatric columnist was Dr. Theodore Rubin, author of *Lisa and David* and many other books in the area of mental health. Dr. Helen deRosis, a psychiatrist specializing in women's depression and anxiety, was another regular writer, always providing a compassionate, wise point of view for women in trouble with themselves and their relationships. In 1980 I added another medical columnist: an internist and cardiologist whose fine writing matched the high quality of his medical credentials. He had done six columns for us when he, too, fell a victim to violence. Surprised by a burglar in his home in the suburbs of Washington, D.C., he was fatally shot, and died chasing his assailant in a car. His name was Dr. Michael Halberstam and it was a cruel and senseless loss.

Mental health was a problem with one of the most gregarious, seemingly bright-spirited women I have ever known: the *Journal*'s long-time etiquette authority Amy Vanderbilt, who died in an accidental fall from her town house window.

It wasn't until after the funeral (the protocol and service had all been planned by her beforehand) that I discovered the long battle this vital woman had waged against depression, an illness that often pushed her into hospitalization. Her book, of course, is still one of the standard works of etiquette. Another good one is by the glamorous and highly creative Charlotte

Ford. *The Amy Vanderbilt* etiquette book now is kept updated and revised by Letitia Baldrige, social adviser to five White Houses, public relations executive, and one of the most truly stylish women I know. Tish, sister of President Reagan's Secretary of Commerce, is still called in on special protocol assignments. She coordinated First Lady attendance at Mrs. Truman's funeral, for example.

Editors and people in the publishing business are always besieged with questions on how to get a book or an article published. The inevitable answer is, get an agent. But this is a copout, since the hot-shot agents like Mort Janklow, Sterling Lord, Scott Meredith, Swifty Lazar, Bill Adler, Lynn Nesbitt, and Julian Bach don't accept unsolicited manuscripts and tend to steer away from unpublished authors. There is a book, *How to Get Happily Published,* by Judith Applebaum and Nancy Evans (New American Library), which is about the most comprehensive guide I've ever seen. It even tells you how to cope with rejection slips. I recommend it.

These days, of course, the big question is, What's going to happen to reading in the whole new world of video and computer technology?

It's a world into which I myself have recently entered. And although microcircuitry remains mystifying (a chip, to me, is still largely something in a chocolate cookie or what you use in a poker game), I have learned a good deal. And I know that our culture is going to be dominated by telecommunications. The groaning board of electronic goods and services will make it harder than ever to find available time between sleep and work. Kids are the most conditioned: Apple, IBM, and other electronic powers have changed the way they count, read, and learn, at home and at school. "Computer literacy will soon be as fundamental to the productive functioning of the average American as the ability to write," says a math professor at the Massachusetts Institute of Technology. Our synapses will be attuned to the screen, and those heavy, cumbersome things we called books may find their doomsday in the "computer-friendly" frame of mind.

Or will they? Will the reading habit wither as more of us sit before that great Lookie Monster, the home terminal, and get our information and our relaxation through an electronic umbilical cord? Will children erase the habit of "print-think" and never know the rhythms of a Shelley or the greatness of a Shakespeare or even the simpler pleasures of a good magazine article, as they tune into the alphanumerics of a database console, or walk around with a headset preparing them for tomorrow's final exam in The History of Satellite Communications?

I am an optimist. Even as I explore the horizons of cable TV and videotex and all kinds of electronic communications, I still maintain my marrow-deep faith in the printed word.

You don't need electricity to read a book or a magazine; there are no blackouts or cutoffs on the fuel known as imagination. You can take a book or magazine on a bus, or curl up with it in bed until it drops from your sleepy fingers. You can prop it up in the kitchen and check a recipe. You can return to a page at any time without punching a keyboard to call up access from the dark heart of a machine. You can share it with a neighbor, clip it, frame it, file it, have it autographed, hoard it until you sell it in a garage sale.

There is bound to be less time for everything, and probably less available money. We all seem to be developing an impatience for anything that takes more than a half-hour (including disasters and wars). But the hunger of human beings to have magazines and books available to them will not fade. Readers are hard to breed out of the species, even with the genetic engineering of modern technology. Magazines and books will continue to be part of the tools and joys of living. Provided, of course, that those of us who believe in the printed word keep giving them not just best-sellers, but best-tellers.

FOUR

The Women's Movement: Seeing the Light

It started like a brush fire in the hills that everyone ignored because it seemed like nothing more than an interesting patch of reflected sunlight.

When it broke into a blaze, there were familiar echoes of the civil rights and peace movements in its crackle. But the real fuel was in the inflammable angers and frustrations of millions of women. Suddenly, there was this stunning possibility that life was stacked against them not only because of a failure of fate or of themselves, but because they were women in a man-controlled society.

Out of the shadows they emerged. Women professionals and students whose career paths had been blocked for reasons of gender. Secretaries who got the coffee and the fanny-pats but never the substantial raises. Middle-aged wives dumped by unfeeling husbands. Single mothers with no place to leave their children when they worked. Women tired of using separate entrances at clubs, of being refused credit cards in their own names, of jokes about "dumb broads" and "chicks."

The list of grievances was as long as the women were varied, ranging from quiet questionings to bread-and-butter and survival issues. Not all women were hit on a sensitive nerve; plenty did not agree. ("Keep your cotton-pickin' hands off my shackles," wrote one *Journal* reader. "I know a good thing when I see it, and I'm hanging on to it.") But enough were awakened and moved and stirred to earn this phenomenon the title of The Women's Movement of the Seventies.

"The women's movement, which started as personal truth, not seen or understood by the experts, or even the women themselves, because it did not fit the accepted image, has in the space of a generation, changed life and the accepted image." So wrote Betty Friedan in her 1981 book *The Second Stage.* Betty Friedan is the long-distance runner of the movement, the original banner-waver *(The Feminine Mystique)* and the thoughtful reappraiser. But even in her latest dogma, as she proposed amnesty between the sexes as the mature way to create equality, she was scorned by both conservatives and radicals, and unforgiven by men because she is not a clone of Mary Tyler Moore or even of Dustin Hoffman's Dorothy Michaels.

Was it all just a phase of the moon, a minority enthusiasm that blew hot and cooled down in the inevitable winter of boredom? Did those female exasperaters really jolt the world into a shift of cultural attitudes? The two stated enemies were not unseated: the System, which most of us were prepared to modify but not to uproot, and Men, who maintained strong outposts in our hearts and heads even as we strove to expose their prejudices. Now, in the eighties, many of the changes are so ingrained that we take them for granted, and the momentum seems to have slowed. But we did come some way, baby, from the original manipulative gentility of "Never Underestimate the Power of a Woman." That famed *Journal* slogan developed modern teeth, even as the magazine itself adapted. And both still have bite.

The Women's Movement: Seeing the Light

Back in the seventies, the women's movement was the town's hot ticket, the new excitement. At urban cocktail parties, the dialectic of Steinem and Millett and Greer was as common as white wine and quiche. TV comedians and sitcoms made hay with caricatures of "libbers" and "bra burners." The press, while minimizing their goals, frontpaged pictures of frowsy, feisty women carrying sisterhood placards. In the executive offices of publishing companies, major corporations, government agencies, and other institutions, personnel policies were carefully reviewed just in case this all became another regulatory crisis.

For me personally, liberation was a complex issue. I was not, after all, battered, bruised, or even visibly disadvantaged. I had a family, an interesting and prestigious job, and a full-time housekeeper. If I had ever been sexually harassed at work, it must have been benign and felt more like a treat than a treatment.

But I knew something was wrong. In spite of the skills I knew I possessed, there were deep holes in my confidence and self-esteem. I literally could not, at that time, get up in front of an audience to speak. Wherever I had worked, I had been a petted child, not an equal. Being No. 2, or further on down the line, had its comfort factor: I didn't have to take the front-line responsibility. And serving as the power behind the throne to a string of male bosses gave me the spice of intrigue and the warmth of being needed.

It was nice. But on the basic levels, I knew I was suffering from a case of personality undernourishment. I wrote their speeches, helped guide their career strategies, brought them my best ideas like burnt offerings, and cheered from the sidelines. At home, I deferred to the importance of my husband's job—he was, after all, a doctor, and that was the essence of life and death. One man I worked for in the early years said it all when he moved elsewhere without me. "You helped a lot.

81

Now I've got to prove I can do it without you." Which he did, and I still cheered from the sidelines.

But none of these men ever encouraged me to advance to their own levels, ever showed me how to develop my career strengths so that I could be more than an adjunct. Until I met a multi-talented man named Edward R. Downe, Jr., who became my first real mentor. No woman, with the exception of longtime friend and financial expert Sylvia Porter, ever urged me to bolster my financial skills, to get to the core of where it was all happening, the balance sheet.

I wasn't exactly a doormat. And I wasn't suffering discrimination in any obvious way. But I took it for granted that even on a woman's magazine, there would be few if any top women executives, that the *Journal* would not think there was anything wrong in having its annual Chicago golf outing at a club where women were banned, and that some of the men I worked with considered all new attractive secretaries fair game for their extramarital fun and games.

For me, it all truly started on the morning of March 18, 1970. That was the day on which 200 militant feminists walked into the office of then editor-in-chief John Mack Carter and staged the famous 11-hour *Ladies' Home Journal* sit-in. It was a stormy, dramatic day that made history. Some say it made John Carter. Nobody has ever spelled out the seismic effects it had on me.

How do I explain that strange, convoluted relationship I had for so many years—first at *McCall's* and then at the *Journal*—with the quick, able, ambitious John Mack Carter? He came to New York a country boy with big-city aspirations. We were close, intuitive friends, and often competitive teammates. The two of us could work a roomful of celebrities like sly pickpockets, frisking everyone for contacts and ideas. We took interest in each other's families, and John and Sharlyn and Sol and Lenore sometimes traveled together—Washington, Puerto Rico, and one unforgettable week at Eleanor Lambert's house in Acapulco. We engineered major feats of magazine involvement, including a trip to the Paris Peace Conference in the middle of the Vietnam war, which I discuss elsewhere. But he was always, despite his trenchant, antic sense of humor, the self-protective domineering boss. And I was the pliant, deferring acolyte. There was no other way. While it fed my masochism, it stunted my growth. The truth is that I invested a lot of secret tears as well as shining hours in John Mack Carter, today editor of *Good Housekeeping* and director of magazine development for Hearst. Even now, when we greet each other warmly, united by memories as well as a lingering sympatico, I find it difficult to assess who was using whom in those early days. I don't know who in the end won that strange game we played a decade or more ago against the background of women's emergence. Perhaps we both won and lost. He took his blows in that delicate male professional ego. My pain was more personal. In that sense, we were a microcosm of it all. And we both survived . . . although I still don't have his picaresque self-confidence.

It seemed like any normal Wednesday. The day before, someone had mentioned the possibility of a women's action. But we dismissed it as an idle rumor. And so I had come in at my regular 8:15 A.M. time from Riverdale, to meet with John, also an early starter, and discuss magazine plans in the works along with the latest office gossip. His big corner office at 641 Lexington Avenue was opulently masculine, deep blue and tobacco-colored, with dark shutters. (Later, I was to change the mood with yellow floral chintz.) I stood in front of his desk, arguing some point about a story. Suddenly, there was a flurry at the office door and the show began. For weeks, John was to hiss at me, "If you hadn't been in my office, the door would have been closed!"

In they streamed, a noisy, motley procession. They were

women of all ages, without makeup, in fashions more *lumpen* than Halston, costumed for revolt. In an office which normally had seating room for a dozen, there suddenly were women everywhere, standing, sitting on the floor, draped over the table and the windowsills, and spilling out into the halls. For the first few moments, they all seemed to shout at once. It was a zoo.

The group represented many feminist organizations, from the more moderate National Organization for Women (NOW) to the New York Radical Feminists to the very radical Redstockings. Some of them carried a big cover mockup in which our logo had been redone to "Women's Liberated Journal," with the illustration of a pregnant woman carrying a picket sign lettered "Unpaid Labor." There were no individual identifications, but among them were Susan Brownmiller, serving as a kind of group leader, Ti-Grace Atkinson, and a friendly young activist named Sookie Stammler. Also present was a disaffected *Journal* editor who had been previously let go. She had thoughtfully provided the front door keys and a map of the entire floor. Everyone had assembled even earlier at St. Peter's Lutheran Church across the street.

The *Village Voice* of March 16 had a report by Minda Bikman which was slanted but detailed.

We found Carter standing by his desk, flanked by Lenore Hershey, his yes-woman and the only female senior editor on staff. A brief look of surprise flicked across his face before he resumed the blank expression which he held for most of the day. Hershey looked around at us as we quickly filled the large square room and her smile came out as a tight little grin. Several of our spokeswomen identified us and the purpose of our early morning visit—we were here to liberate a magazine, read by an estimated 14 million women, from the content it purveys. We demanded an issue as reparation for all the money spent by American women paying these editors' salaries. The spokeswomen also read a statement demanding Carter's resignation and an end to the magazine as it now exists, both in the structure of the book and in the structure of the staff. We were there to destroy a publication which feeds off women's anger and frustration, a magazine which destroys women.

The reasons for choosing the *Journal* were obvious: its name, its eighty-seven-year history, its seeming preoccupation with the homemaker—although we had already made arrangements to run Letty Cottin Pogrebin's "Working Woman" column.

But John Carter was also a perfect foil. Compact, cocky, forty-one, John with his clenched pipe and his boyish good looks was one of the most charismatic figures in the magazine business. He was born in Kentucky, half of a male-female twin pair, and nine months with a sister *in utero* may have left an imprint. John didn't like to be crowded by anyone, especially women. And here were 200 of them, threatening, nagging, shouting, imprisoning him behind his desk, and for the first few minutes anyway providing him with one of the most shattering experiences of his life. He did have a blank expression, I remember, and I must have also had a tight, tense grin.

As yes-woman (and Lady Friday, as I was referred to in another newspaper) I moved in behind the desk close to him, tapping his shoe with mine for reassurance. I also womanned the phone, which could not be shut off. An executive downstairs asked if we wanted to call the police. The answer was no. Shana Alexander, who was then, briefly, the editor of *McCall's*, telephoned to ask if she could come over with sandwiches. I clobbered that one. This was *our* sit-in and we weren't about to share it with our chief rival.

And then the reporters and the TV cameras started to roll in and we realized what this was all about. It was show-and-tell time, and all the newspapers, wire services, and TV stations had been tipped off, with the request that only women be assigned to the story. But both sexes turned up. One black male reporter for NBC came into the crowded room and was dismissed so insultingly that he said to his tormentor, "You should be glad you're a woman. If you were a man, you'd be down on the floor."

I wasn't really frightened, although they booed me, too, calling me a token woman, every time I tried to make a calm statement. As the first hour passed, John began to regain some of his poise, perching on the edge of his desk. This infuriated some of the women who had been hanging large posters out of the normally sealed windows reading "Women Unite—Join Us" and *"Ladies' Home Journal* Liberated." Twice during this early period, as he protested "I will not negotiate," they tried to push him off his desk, and also threatened to throw him out the window. But more prudent forces dominated. Actually, if it had become any more violent, I had a secret plan. I was going to do the Victorian maneuver of falling to the floor in a dead faint. It would have worked. They would have said insulting things as they called a doctor or an ambulance, but they would have called. Fortunately, I did not have to use this diversion.

At about 11:00 A.M., we started to negotiate. The *Village Voice* again: "Carter and Hershey worked like a team, with Carter dropping one line hints and Hershey megaphoning them out, although we all knew of course what Carter was saying."

The protesters then came up with their article ideas: "How to Get an Abortion," "A Prostitute Talks to Her Client's Wife," "How Women Are Kept Apart":

As the talks bogged down in a hash of Carter-Hershey doubletalk, it became a question of who would tire first— but there were only two of them and many of us and we were prepared to stay overnight. Becoming disgusted with Carter-Hershey's routine, one woman suggested we should remain silent. "Look," she said, "he hasn't said a word all day. She does all the talking for him. How do you think it would look to the women of America when they find out that the *Journal* editor can't even talk to women?"

This part of the *Village Voice* piece I never discussed with John. Symptomatically, it made *me* feel guilty. The demonstrators demanded a full issue for their message; we rejected it. We offered a general article on the movement; they rejected it. Finally we decided that we would give them a section of the August *Journal,* provided we would have some control over what went in, and they agreed, with a double veto in case we used too much control. I was nominated as negotiator, begrudgingly, and the final wrap-up did not take place until after 5:00 P.M. By then they had smoked the cigars on John's desk, taken over the men's room, and left the editorial offices in a mess. There was still some talk of staying overnight, but somebody—I seem to remember it was Susan Brownmiller— had a hair appointment. Wearily, we closed up shop and everyone on both sides rushed to watch the TV news and wait for tomorrow's newspapers, all of which were generous in their coverage.

It was not an isolated event. *Newsweek* had recently been the scene of an action in which forty-six women staffers mailed a government protest charging the magazine with bypassing women as writers. But the *Journal*'s sit-in got a big play everywhere. Even the advertising trade was alerted; after all, the women had attacked ads as being demeaning, too.

Advertising Age the following week carried a write-up in which the *Journal*'s ad director, Bob Lucas, was quoted as saying that while the magazine did not have women among its 32 sales representatives, "if a woman was qualified and proved to be superior to a man who came in for a rep job, I'd be foolish not to take her." But he pointed out that there could be "some prejudice" from male clients whom the women called on. (Remember, this was not 1870 . . . it was 1970.)

The same item pointed out that *McCall's, Good Housekeeping,* and *Woman's Day* didn't have female reps, either. *Cosmo* did, but their publisher condescendingly added that they did particularly well in areas in which they were interested, like jewelry and cosmetics.

Today, of course, the picture is changed. The *Journal* broke the ice by hiring irrepressible, unflagging Suzanne Douglas (she now owns and runs *Intro Magazine)* who proceeded to sell circles around many of the males on the staff. Much later, Carol Taber moved into a sales manager slot and left to become advertising director and associate publisher of *Working Woman.* On most women's magazines today, women are a good percentage of the sales force.

The following week, in the second floor conference room, we got down to the business of planning the section, with Hershey as negotiator in an all-female group. The women worked as a collective, with their own lawyer. For the first time in my life, I got the feel of what it was like to have control of a situation, to be in charge. The women activists by now had my sympathy, and I did not want them to throw away the opportunity, both for themselves and for the magazine. But I was also determined not to indulge their sometimes muddle-headed ignorance about how a magazine works. So rules were set up and a price established: $10,000 for the section, to be split up among the groups however they saw fit. Some of the factions wanted more. The new Hershey stood firm.

"We'll take it to *McCall's*," some of them threatened. "Be my guest," I responded, handing them the phone. They backed down.

And then Susan Brownmiller committed what I consider was an act of hypocrisy and betrayal. She absented herself from the proceedings and went upstairs to the seventh floor to flirt with Dick Kaplan (today he is the able editor of *US* magazine). He called me on the interoffice phone.

"Can't we give them just a little more?" he wheedled, with Susan undoubtedly beside him using tactics that were more seductively feminine than crisply feminist.

"Absolutely not," I answered. "And Dick, you male chauvinist, stay out of it. *I'm* handling this."

The eight-page section which ran in the August issue on blue-green stock does not seem particularly shocking in current terms. Its articles were long, discursive, dull: "Babies Are Born, Not Delivered," "Women Talk About Love and Sex," "Women and Work," "How to Start Your Own Conciousness-Raising Group." Besides eliminating some street language and making normal copy corrections, the *Journal* made no major revisions. A list was also provided of liberation groups across the country which interested readers could contact.

The opening page was a message from John Mack Carter. It was a fine piece of writing that both explained and disclaimed, ending:

This is 1970. All peoples and both sexes are free to examine their own roles . . . to find dignity and self-fulfillment on their own terms. The new movement . . . could even triumph over its man-hating bitterness and indeed win humanist gains for all women—and their men.

John Carter not only liked the resonance of these words, he also seemed to believe them. Suddenly, there he was, the Bronxville hero of the siege of the sit-in, the new prophet of social change. On TV, radio, and podiums across the country, he became a sought-after celebrity. The August section did not bring instant approval from *Journal* readers. Almost half were violently anti, although surprisingly, 54 percent ranged from mild disapproval to cheers. But the *Journal* in the trade press was still perceived as a "sugar and spice" magazine for the bound-in-tradition homemaker. Even the *Wall Street Journal* of the period discounted any possibility of the magazine moving into the future.

The press has always had a curled-lip, peevish attitude toward women's magazines—a kind of automatic mother-identification which brings out the adolescent hostility in both male and female reporters. Yes, homemakers were the main target of women's magazines for decades, but that was before women, and homemakers, and society itself achieved the diversity they have now. Perhaps there were not that many dramatic changes in the *Journal* in the months after the sit-in. But as John moved up into management, and as I became more and more involved in the planning of the magazine, there were subtle alterations.

In 1972, for example, the *Journal* had such cover lines as "What to Do If Your Boss Discriminates Against Women," "How to Be a Better Sex Partner," "How I Won the Fight to Be the First Woman Rabbi." Amy Vanderbilt recognized the new etiquette: what you do when your male guest brings his mistress to your home. (Don't use the old-fashioned word "mistress," and give them separate rooms after discussing it with the woman involved.) Also, how to handle older parents shocked by the new permissive language and earthy stories. (Tell them to be tolerant and not to wince; each previous generation is shocked by the new one.) Under the feature heading "The Power of a Woman" I went to Chicago, and reported (as well as ran) a luncheon honoring hundreds of women leaders and activists in business, politics, environmentalism, education, and volunteerism.

Early in 1973, my campaign to advance took a forward step. I was made executive editor of the *Journal*. And then in October of that year, poker-player John Carter went for a royal flush and uncharacteristically dealt himself a cold hand.

John had been playing high-power politics at Downe Publishing. Ed Downe had given him full authority, plus a limousine and driver to match his own, plus all sorts of financial arrangements which were rumored to be astronomic. John was deeply involved in total management. But in the fall of 1972, as both editor of the *Journal* and Downe's chairman of the board, John started negotiating with the Chicago-based Pritzkers, who were buying *McCall's*. They had noticed his high visibility and his willful enticement of advertising and circulation dollars, and wanted John to run the new operation. Everything about the deal was supposed to be highly confidential when the story broke in *The New York Times*. Since John supposedly had a contract with a no-compete clause, the shock wave moved across the publishing world. Both sides turned against John, and for about a week, he holed up in his office incommunicado. We knew that eventually he would fall through the trapdoor into a field of daisies. As he did.

But it was obvious that he would have to vacate the editorship. And that I had a choice. I could either wait for another male to whom I could genuflect. Or I could strike out for the job myself.

Which I did. I organized the staff and made my pitch to Ed Downe, who was tough, fair, and encouraging. I became editor of *Ladies' Home Journal* in November 1973, and the January 1974 issue was the first one with my name on it as editor. It was also the first issue in the smaller size, but that had been planned years before.

And so I became the first solo woman editor of *Ladies' Home Journal* since its founding mother, Louisa Knapp Curtis, began the magazine almost a century ago. Ironically, among all the congratulatory letters, telegrams, flowers, and telephone calls was not one word from anyone who had been at the sit-in. I did not mind. My "tight little grin" had turned into the last laugh.

FIVE

Women: Moving On

Being editor of *Ladies' Home Journal* for eight shining, success-ful years was a big-time adventure for me. In my lap were all the responsibilities—words, graphics, fiction, articles, service, covers, cover lines, cartoons, everything. I wanted to be true to the magazine's great heritage of civilized tradition. But I knew it was a new bra-less, living-together, microwave age, in which the internal values as well as the exterior trappings were changing. The *Journal*, like its audience, had to move on.

When I took over, it was still a big deal for a woman to be in charge. Was I going to make it, or fall on my derriere because the old boy network was right and it took the management muscle of a man to keep (oops!) all those balls up in the air?

The question crossed my mind. But once on the job, there was no time for gender-preening.

With some exceptions. As a women's magazine editor, I know it helps to have been there. You know intimacy from the inward-sloping side of the bed, the difference between having sex and making love. You've felt the wound of such simple declarative sentences as "Mommy, my teacher wants to see you," "We're going to take a biopsy," "I hate to bother you at work, but there's a lake in the basement." You've faced such

93

enemies as three-way mirrors, gray hairs in your brush, and freezers that break down the day before a party. You can discuss breast-feeding, orgasms, and toxic shock without looking, as some male editors do, as if you've wandered into the wrong locker room.

You have not met all your readers, but you have a sense of kinship with them. You know their aspirations and their confusions. You feel their loneliness, their need to be appreciated, their desire to be better. And if your empathy is slipped in, like honey and spice, between the covers, they know it's there.

I also wondered how the staff would react as I stepped into the footprints of my male predecessor. Would that team of assorted, temperamental, talented personalities accept a Big Mommy instead of a Big Daddy?

The matriarchal parallel gave me my clue. Male editors had taught me much. But I could not imitate the brooding intellectual paternalism of Bob Stein at *McCall's*. As for Maestro Herbert R. Mayes (I never could get around to calling him Herb) there was no way I could match his perfectionist, tyrannical father image. Today in his eighties, the dean of all women's magazine editors, he was once cited by a writer as "running a magazine like the overseer of a chain gang." Let's be fair. If Mr. Mayes was pleased, he would occasionally remove your chains and feed you bonbons.

Instinctively, I did it my way. Conferences were moved from behind the barrier of the desk into the living room part of my office. My door stayed unsecretively open unless someone came in to tell me the company was about to be sold, to complain about a salary, or seemed on the verge of tears. (Once in a while, the door was hastily shut because I knew *I* was about to cry.)

The day I really, truly assumed command was a few weeks after the official date, when three staff members appeared as a dissident group to question a layout decision I had made.

"Why does it have to be this way?" they demanded. Although I can be cracker-crisp when the occasion demands it, Dragon Lady was never my role. The old me would have felt compelled to explain and conciliate. But the time had come to define the territory. As I did when my daughter was small, limits had to be set.

"Because I am the editor and I want it that way," I said firmly.

There was no small pool of guilt dripping from sweaty fingers. No clutch of fear that they'd all walk out on me. Inside my psyche, everything fell coolly into place. As it did in all the offices up and down the hall. I had found my management style.

The *Journal* at that period was a healthy institution, still in its glory, still making lots of money. So I did not feel the need to make any dramatic editorial changes. But, as I said, a lot of things were happening out there, especially to and for women. The working women phenomenon was spreading like wildfire. Out in the hinterlands, homemakers with curlers in their hair were reading *Ms.* magazine and spilling baby formula on their paperback copies of *The Feminine Mystique.* Our reader mail was beginning to reveal new evidences of candor and restlessness:

"I have a husband and two great children. Yet I am haunted by this feeling that my life has not yet begun."

"We're both working now, and I don't know exactly what's happening to my marriage."

"I don't hate men, but I'm tired of being a second-class citizen."

Having your consciousness raised was conventional wisdom at this period, and I was no exception. I saw discrimination against women with new eyes, and I saw it in a lot of places. In my own marriage, success on my side had brought subtle differences, too, which required some mutual adjustment. (He says *he* adjusted. I say I did most of the bending.) I was suspicious of hard-line feminist dogma, but underneath it was an emerging truth which I felt the *Journal* should recognize and support, as a natural continuation of its crusading history.

But how? We weren't *Ms.* and our audience of 14 million women wasn't about to storm the barricades on women's issues. Over a long lunch, Sylvia Porter and I brainstormed about how the *Journal* could most effectively find its place in the women's movement. It was she who convinced me that the way to go was to get more actively involved in money management and financial recognition, where the freedom and power and independence started. We also both agreed that it was better not just to proselytize among the women themselves, but to do some convincing at the top of the power structure, where the shots were being called. If my more radical friends accused me of consorting with the enemy or moving from grassroots to big league show-biz, it did not faze me. I felt, as I still feel, that the women's movement lost out by constantly talking only to itself, and not also reaching out to the unconverted.

Richard Nixon was still in the White House. At Sylvia's suggestion, I went down to see Herb Stein, the economics professor who was then chairman of the President's Council of Economics, an awesome bear of a man with a dry sense of humor hidden like a minty surprise in his austerity. I asked him if he would write an article on women's new role in the economy. What he subsequently submitted was a dry, sexist report that would have been a bore even in an accountants' trade journal.

I called him on the phone and chided him for being so out of sync with the real world. Out of that conversation came a new article and a whole new government committee, on which I served. And for the first time in history, a chapter on women in the President's 1973 Economic Report. It also led to my structuring of a major San Francisco seminar on women in the economy, cosponsored by the *Journal* and the Bank of America. Herb Stein opened it and paid me a gold-standard compliment.

He explained to the topflight audience of women how I had attacked his first draft, and been responsible for his regeneration. He ended by saying: "So if one brand has been saved from the burning, if one male chauvinist pig has been koshered, the responsibility goes to Mrs. Hershey."

The bandwagon moved on, in women's groups and in high places. In 1974, President Ford formed the President's National Commission for the Observance of International Women's Year, inviting Pat Carbine of *Ms.* and me as women's magazine representatives.

In the same period, an idea of mine that I had fostered for years came into being. It was the *Ladies' Home Journal* Women of the Year honors, which extended women's awards far beyond bathing suit parades and beauty contests. Against the glittering background of the brand-new John F. Kennedy Center in Washington, D.C., we launched what was to become an institution, an exciting, splashy but sound recognition of women, based on our readers' own votes, with a blue-ribbon jury doing the final selection to achieve balance and avoid the tilt of write-ins. With pursestrings unfettered, Clairol was the original sponsor; Procter and Gamble picked up the TV bills for the second two years. Joe Cates was the producer, and I served as executive producer, with the responsibilities of rounding up the big names for the show, as well as hand-holding, script-approving, and general mothering.

Our premiere was a black-tie, live presentation on CBS—TV prime time. What a star-spangled night! The awardees were Dr. Virginia Apgar, anesthesiology specialist in the newborn; Congresswoman Shirley Chisholm; the black poet Nikki Giovanni; publishing executive Katherine Graham; Indian activist Ladonna Harris; actress Helen Hayes; philanthropist Mary Lasker, and voluntary action leader Ellen Sulzberger Straus.

Rosalind Russell, still magnificent though puffy-faced from the treatments for her painful arthritis, served as hostess, and even lured her good friend Mamie Eisenhower up on stage for a touching tribute. The audience was packed with notables, too: Henry Kissinger, the Muskies, the Harrimans, and a lot of other Washington biggies. Onstage, Helen Reddy sang her Grammy-winning hit "I Am Woman," and Sandy Duncan and Jack Klugman won laughs in a skit about the first woman astronaut and her reluctant father. In millions of homes across the country, we were making a statement. We also rang up smashing ratings.

Women of the Year was to be a mega-production for seven years, predating the musical *Woman of the Year*, which was actually based on an old Katharine Hepburn movie. Katharine Houghton Hepburn was one of the few awardees who chose not to be present for her acceptance. She wrote me a note saying, "It is my policy to be ungracious." (She also boycotted Oscar award ceremonies.) Later, she wrote me another letter, thanking me for her pin.

Women of the Year moved from Kennedy Center to Lincoln Center in New York, with even more glamour and excitement. Another year, we took over the Ford Theater in Washington, D.C. There were always gala parties, too. A unique setting was at Cartier's. Here on the main floor of this expensive New York jewelry shop, such stars as Beverly Sills and Carol Burnett drank champagne between the diamonds.

98

The only woman who actually declined the award was the 1977 Nobel Prize-winner in medicine, Dr. Rosalyn Yalow, who claimed it was a "ghetto award" because it was restricted to women. Dr. Yalow and I debated the issue on the Op-Ed pages of *The New York Times* and elsewhere. On the actual night of the awards, in which we also honored Lady Bird Johnson, her former press secretary, Liz Carpenter, was queried about the absent Dr. Yalow's views. "I think she'd better get her nose out of a test tube," said women's equality fighter Liz.

There were always crises. In 1975, author Lillian Hellman received an award, presented by Helen Hayes who, because of a strained ligament, came to the theater on crutches. I picked Ms. Hellman up myself in a cab (she didn't want a limo), and she was fuming about the preceding evening's Academy Awards. (Burt Schneider, producer of the anti-Vietnam documentary "Hearts and Minds," had read a telegram from Hanoi on the Oscar show. Bob Hope and Frank Sinatra, seemingly speaking for the Academy, disavowed his point of view.) When Lillian Hellman received our Woman of the Year award, she was just supposed to make a short acceptance speech. Instead, on live network TV, she continued the fracas by lacing into Sinatra and Hope. The executives in the control booth tore their hair out at this unnecessary bit of controversy. But knowing Lillian Hellman, nobody should have been surprised.

The tensest night was in 1976. We were at the Ed Sullivan Theater on Broadway. The network was NBC. The sponsor, Procter and Gamble. NBC technicians were in the middle of a bitter strike, and the theater was ringed by noisy pickets, who cared not that we were on the side of the angels. Pearl Bailey, a presenter, leaned out of a side window and pleaded with them to go away.

The climax of the show was supposed to be an award to

First Lady Betty Ford. All day, there were calls to and from the White House, assessing the security situation. It was not until the Secret Service arrived with the bomb-sniffing dogs (stupidly, I thought there was someone blind in the rehearsal house) that our hopes really rose. Yes, Betty Ford was coming, and it was her birthday, too. To match this dramatic event, we had arranged to have Elizabeth Taylor (who, since she had not yet married John Warner, was still not a Republican) wheel out a birthday cake. At five o'clock, four hours before air time, I was notified by her press secretary that Mrs. Ford would prefer not to have Elizabeth Taylor do the birthday cake bit. While our producer and the ratings-predictors groaned, to me fell the job of disinviting Elizabeth Taylor. The tremors could be felt throughout Manhattan. Meanwhile, the pickets, persuaded by their leaders, graciously moved out of the way so Betty Ford would not have to cross the picket line, hostess Barbara Walters calmed everybody down, and the show went on. Kate Smith sang "God Bless America," the Fifth Dimension did their thing, and Pearl Bailey and Mrs. Ford danced together for the photographers. It was another triumph . . . for the *Journal*, but also for women.

In 1979, we enlarged the concept to "A Celebration of Women" and named eleven Women of the Decade and ten Women of the Future. We taped this one for syndication, fortunately. It was a sit-down, black-tie dinner at the Hotel Pierre, in which somehow the seating arrangements went awry, and everyone was convinced they had been exiled to Siberia. Once more, the women awardees and their presenters saved the day. Phyllis George Brown, ever so slightly pregnant, played First Mother of Kentucky all over the place. Marlo Thomas, First Feminist, was surprisingly polite to Marie Osmond, who looked pained whenever someone made a reference to ERA. Cheryl Tiegs and Ali McGraw acquitted themselves well, and Erma Bombeck flew in from Phoenix to do her usual funny number in introducing her friend Sylvia Porter. Barbara Walters, almost an anchorwoman on our Women of the Year shows, received her Woman of the Decade award from Hugh Downs. But the biggest hit of the evening was singer Marian Anderson. This great black woman, now in her eighties, spoke with striking dignity of her fight to achieve, and she spontaneously gave some of the credit to *Ladies' Home Journal,* which she read as a girl. One of the women we honored as a Woman of the Future was stunner Sherry Lansing, then a vice-president of Columbia Pictures. In a few weeks, she became president of Twentieth Century-Fox, where she ruled until her resignation early this year to take on still another big assignment.

It was another glorious, inspiring, and star-studded evening. When it hit the air a few weeks later, it rang up respectable ratings. Unfortunately, it was the last show of its kind. I hope someone will revive Women of the Year either for network or for cable. These awards did much to focus national interest on women's accomplishments, and they also provided young women with role models. I differ sincerely with Dr. Yalow about the negative value of women's awards. As I said at the time, "when 51.3 percent of the Nobel prizes are women, I will agree that such prizes are old-fashioned."

If one is mugged, crime becomes an uppermost issue. If one is as exposed as I was to many previously unnoticed evidences of sexual prejudice and discrimination, the issue of women's rights becomes paramount. Some of my reaction was personal: I saw in a new light my own habits of conforming to other wills. Some of it was anger at the big and small blocks unjustly put in women's way simply because of their sex. It may have been a little late to change the world for me, but I could help others. I was carrying a heavy load, at the office and at home. But I could always squeeze more in, and I was in a unique spot to make a contribution. Not to use my opportunity would have been wasteful.

The mid-seventies were a time of committees, commissions, and task forces; sometimes I feel we all talked ourselves to death. I went to monthly meetings in Washington with the I.W.Y. Commission, learned how parliamentary procedure can be used to promote the views of the skillful, met all the Big Names in feminism, Republican and Democrat. Most of them were dedicated women, but one of my fellow commissioners was Alan Alda, then already a star in TV's *M*A*S*H*. Alan, like my confrère, Sey Chassler, editor of *Redbook*, was a zealot about the feminist cause. In its behalf, he would lend his presence cheerfully. Alan Alda made a ringing statement on one of our Women of the Year shows about how freeing women would free men. I always found it amusing that while we sat through those long hours in the meeting rooms, decrying the constant emphasis on women as sex symbols, Alan's dry wit and virile magnetism obviously stirred up some feminine fantasies even among us.

Alan would probably deny this. He disliked facing the fact that his usefulness as a Movement spokesperson had anything to do with his visibility as a male heartthrob. He once did not talk to me for months because I had the temerity to ask his wife, Arlene, an able writer and professional photographer, if she would break a family rule and do a piece on her husband, something Alan considered close to binding her feet and turning her into a concubine. Arlene got up and walked out of my office abruptly, on unbound feet. Many months later, the Hersheys and the Aldas found themselves together at a Philharmonic concert at Lincoln Center. Alan, after first snubbing me, then went into a diatribe about how I had been a traitor to the feminist cause, had hurt both Arlene and him, and would never get another Alda story.

When Sol looked puzzled about what the fuss was all about, Alan turned to him with Hawkeye annoyance.

"You don't know what it's like to be married to a famous person," he told my husband in a voice that would chill wine.

"Yes, I do," answered Sol with an ironic grin of his own. P.S. We patched it up and eventually did get other Alda stories.

I also got to know the four congressional members on our committee: Senators Birch Bayh and Charles Percy, and Representatives Bella Abzug and Margaret Heckler.

If you said "Battling Bella," everybody knew whom you meant. Hat-addicted, razor-tongued Bella Abzug was the congresswoman from New York, a graduate of my own Hunter College, a lawyer, and an ardent liberal and feminist.

Over the span of two commissions, Bella and I became friendly, although I think she found my politics too bland for her taste. Once I rode down on the Washington shuttle with her, and by happenstance I ended up seated between Bella and Ted Kennedy, the epitome of being caught between a rock and a hard place. I switched seats so the two Democratic powerhouses could caucus together, and shamelessly eavesdropped. Like a couple of merchants in the Casbah, they were trading support on some upcoming bills.

Bulk and abrasiveness were Abzug trademarks. I could do nothing about the latter, but to help her health and her image, I once made her a reckless offer. If she would lose fifty pounds on a special *Ladies' Home Journal* diet, I would put her picture on the cover. I never had to face the possibility. As her political fortunes sagged, so did Bella. She gave up her congressional seat for an unsuccessful try at the Senate, then lost out to Ed Koch when she made a bid for the New York mayoralty. And she could not control her nervous eating until much later.

(Today, she's still fighting the weight battle and still in the ring for liberal causes.)

I like Bella's spunk, and perhaps that made her bark at me less often than she did at most people. She also once made a long trip to Riverdale to present me with a local award. But along with many others, I eventually became disenchanted with her tirades, and some of the rash judgments into which her voracious ego pushed her. I agree with what some of her close staff members told me: Bella had the habit of becoming her own worst enemy.

But I supported her when she asked the commission to back a bill proposing a national women's conference to be held as part of the Bicentennial celebration. The bill passed, and $5 million was granted by Congress to the project. When Jimmy Carter became President, he expanded the I.W.Y. Commission, adding to its roster Gloria Steinem, Eleanor Smeal of NOW, Erma Bombeck, and *All in the Family* star Jean Stapleton. He reappointed me as well, and added two male commissioners, John Mack Carter and Sey Chassler. And instead of giving Bella Abzug the Cabinet position for which she was hoping, he proffered the seat as presiding officer of the Commission. She hesitated, but took the job because she needed a national platform. The November 1977 National Women's Conference in Houston, Texas, as well as the fifty-six-state-and-territory meetings which preceded it, became a major focus of activity for all of us who worked on it.

The Houston Conference. Its veterans recall it as World War I old-timers remembered the Battle of the Marne, or perhaps the way someone with an old-school tie evokes the greatest class reunion of them all. "Were you at the Houston conference?" you will ask someone who probably was part of the women's movement in the late seventies. If the answer is affirmative, you will exchange vivid memories which probably don't match. Because this sprawling, vibrant convention in which twenty thousand women (and some men) assembled to lay down resolutions and recommend actions was many things to many people. "We were an all-women Carl Sandburg poem come to life," wrote Lindsy Van Gelder in a *Ms.* piece over-optimistically titled "Four Days That Changed the World." For conservative Phyllis Schlafly and her followers meeting across town amidst Bibles and American flags, it was Sodom and Gomorrah in the not-so-early stages. To me at the time, it was an awe-inspiring effort that somehow got out of hand.

I guess I saw the handwriting on the wall early, when Bella appointed Jean O'Leary, former nun and co-executive director of the National Gay Task Force, to the Commission. One had to be a political virgin, or look like a backward bigot, to protest this publicly, although I considered having some buttons printed up saying "Gay's OK, but there are others in the fray." I have never felt that the personal sexual preference of lesbians should interfere with their human rights, and I understood how oppression and discrimination had contributed to their political drive. But knowing the mood of the mass women's audience out there, I felt that the emphasis on lesbian rights was dangerous to the women's movement. In the end, I believe, it helped to bring it down, right on its axis.

"This is a time for foot soldiers, not kamikaze pilots," thundered Texas Congresswoman Barbara Jordan, another former Woman of the Year, as she delivered the keynote speech in Houston. I sat behind her on the platform and saw her gazing at the balcony where hundreds of self-proclaimed gay women waved balloons lettered "We Are Everywhere" and placards too explicit for TV screens. But kamikaze pilots they were, sacrificing the majority and the ERA amendment to those suicide moments of triumph, handing Schlafly and her followers a negative banner to wave for years to come. My anger was not with those passionate outsiders wanting in. I was

105

mostly peeved with the knowing manipulators at secret cau-
cuses behind the scene, using this mandate to run the show.
Unfortunately, they were also scorching the earth for women
with equally as urgent needs. Even as I thrilled to the heart-
lifting unities of the conference, the Olympic-echoing torch
relay, the fervent phalanx of First Ladies, the many evidences
of diversity blended into sisterhood, I knew the world would
not be changed that quickly.

And it wasn't, although ground was gained. Today we see
women in some significant jobs where they never were before.
We have Sandra Day O'Connor on our highest bench although only 5 percent of total judgeships are held by women.
Pep-packed Peg Heckler is in the Cabinet as Secretary of
Health and Human Services, and we have Elizabeth H. Dole
as Secretary of Transportation. There is a sprinkling of able
women in every level of government, although most of us
would like to see many more moving up the political ladder.

The traditional women's magazines—dubbed the Seven
Sisters, after the Ivy League women's colleges—have largely
changed their approach and their tone of voice. No longer is
there just an expectable stream of hairdos, hamburger recipes,
and cheery solutions to domestic travail. Today these magazines address all the choices and the options and the dilemmas
of the modern woman: to stay at home or to work, to have
children now or postpone, to hang on to a bad marriage or to
face divorce. Threading their way through the conflict of old
values and new opportunities, they have updated their help-
fulness to the new realities, with women editors at the helm as
a matter of course. (When the few remaining male editors-in-
chief depart, females will now have the advantage as their
replacements. The advantage . . . but not a lock on the job.)

What about the constituency that is the most obvious bene-
ficiary of it all: the corporate climbers? The New Women, as
opposed to us retroactive Old Women, aim for the top with

high hopes and revved-up energy. They talk of support systems and networks. They dress for success in expensive suits and tote their status Bottega Veneta carryalls. And yet, when a majority of women officers of America's major companies were recently polled, most said they agreed in principle with the women's movement, but were not psychologically involved. They forgot how quickly scenarios can change.

Bella Abzug went on from the Conference to bait and batter Jimmy Carter, and lost her appointment. She was replaced by Lynda Johnson Robb, who despite begrudging support from the feminists did an effective job.

Bella's blast-offs helped clear the path for a new administration in which women's issues have sunk to the bottom of the priority list. And recent budget cuts hit hardest at families headed by women.

The Equal Rights Amendment, for which so many of us worked so hard, and which was at one time considered a shoo-in, didn't make it. Sad for women. More tragic still for a nation not yet willing to enshrine the fundamental rights of more than half its population.

Women today still earn only 64 cents to every dollar earned by a man. Affirmative action wilts in a negative economy. Husbands recognize the changing role of women to the extent that they enjoy the extra paycheck and the sense of partnership. But deep down they're dubious, especially if a wife goes on too many sales trips, or leaps into a higher-than-his salary bracket. Household chores and parenting duties are only sparingly shared. According to most surveys, the theme song of the American male is still "don't rock the boat."

Legalized abortion is being threatened by the so-called "pro-life" factions. I feel that abortion is a complex moral dilemma oversimplified by both sides. An abortion is always a difficult, tortured decision. A woman will opt for this medical procedure as a last-ditch alternative to bringing into the world an unwanted human who will be sentenced at birth to, most likely, a life of physical or emotional deprivation. For many people, religious precepts are involved, and that's fine. Let them practice what they believe; let them work through churches and synagogues and family education to turn back the sexual revolution. But who has the right to *deny* this other kind of life-protection to those who require it or want it? To me, abortion is basically a matter of personal conscience and social responsibility—and should not be used as a political football.

Not a flamboyant doctrinaire, rational Elizabeth Janeway writes insightfully on women's issues. In a recent book, *Cross Section,* she notes that the women's movement of the past years has been the beginning of a testament "in which we have gotten asfar as the Book of Exodus, or getting out."

But, she adds, "We still have to map the new territory and settle the land and work out the human laws for living there."

True. We all eventually come to grips with the fact that nothing is perfect or complete. Liberation has had its price tags along with its golden credit cards. Some women have traded dependence for lonely bed-and-boredom, some have learned that a job can be as soul-starving as housework. Some stil cling contentedly to vicarious living, "my husband's job," "my husband's trips." (Hopefully not "my husband's pretty new executive assistant.") A recent Bryn Mawr College study shows a surprising swing in emotional emphasis. Seventy-two percent of the youngest women wanted families, most feeling women with small children should not work.

But we still must resist the people who would turn the clock back. There are those conservatives who insist that if we would all just return to old-fashioned values inside a closed circle of people like ourselves, all the terrible things would go away: teenage pregnancy, drugs, crime, child abuse, dirty books and movies, divorce. These social receders aren't very realistic. Because we are forced to deal with what we have, including the rights and freedoms of people who are different from us, as well as people who are like ourselves. Including women, who *can* find ways to incorporate self-fulfillment into family life.

We can't afford to stay aloof and psychologically uninvolved. True, there are big, big problems nationally and internationally that make this issue seem like less of a priority. But it still is crucially important. There will never be a better time to work up a new head of steam for a women's movement with new leaders and new verve.

Let's hope we will be smarter, wiser, less selfish. Maybe this time we'll speak to the needs of all women, and not let fears and hostilities get out of control.

Maybe this time we won't blow it.

SIX

Star Dazzle

For seven years, from 1974 to 1981, I did an annual stint on the *Merv Griffin Show*, handing out *Ladies' Home Journal* awards to top female performers. (Young Ricky Schroeder was the one male exception.) Since I did not want these show-biz tributes to be confused with the more substantive *Ladies' Home Journal* Women of the Year honors, I came up with a title Merv also approved. I called them Star Dazzle Awards. My daughter disapproved. "How rhinestony can you get?" she mocked.

Star dazzle, like the rays of the sun, is best when exposure is moderated. For me, I got my first intense dose during the childhood Saturday afternoons I spent at the local Loew's movie house. (In the Bronx, we pronounced it Low-ese.) With my polo coat folded like a lump in my lap, and a mouthful of fruity jujubes gluing my back teeth together, I was carried away into another world. Stars were really stars then, larger than life, to be worshiped from afar. My heart soared down to Rio with Fred and Ginger, fluttered for the strong-jawed strength of Gable, melted for Garbo's camellia beauty.

But best of all was the femme fatale glamour of Joan Crawford. Her moist-eyed, lush-lipped, husky-voiced charisma was irresistible. And those clothes, broad-shouldered and dramatic, were everything a thirties teenager would consider the ultimate in chic. Joan had just married that charmer with the crooked smile, Franchot Tone, and I felt that if I could ever find a male that effortlessly engaging while he smoked a pipe with the bowl upside down, as Tone did in some windy naval epic of the period, I would have met my Mr. Right. (Years later, I did meet a man who puffed a briar. When he tried smoking it upside down, the tobacco fell out.)

The tape moved fast-forward, and my magazine career put me within reaching distance of the celebrity world. Part of me was still the star-struck girl, caught up in the heady fantasy of those towering personalities who lived in far-off Hollywood and were unlike the prosaic people I knew. The part, fortunately, was the hard-nosed journalist trying to get a story.

We now segue to the early 1960s, when I was doing my "Sight & Sound" column for *McCall's*, interviewing every performer I could grab. Joan Crawford by that time was living alone in Manhattan, in the top floor duplex Fifth Avenue apartment she had moved into when she married businessman Al Steele, Pepsi-Cola's chairman. It had been perhaps the happiest period of her life, but the bubble burst when he died suddenly in 1959. Joan went into a decline. She was already getting a reputation for drinking too much, dozing on the dais as she attended luncheons and dinners, and having difficulty with her grown children, although that did not come out until later. It was the twilight of Joan Crawford, which ended with her death in 1977.

I think I went to visit her in connection with a film, one of those horror—and horrid—movies she did to make money and keep herself before the klieg lights. The meeting had not been too difficult to arrange. At the specified time, I presented myself at the door of her apartment.

The door was opened by a woman I took to be the maid. She was tall and pale, wearing an undistinguished blouse and green slacks. A scarf was tied over drab braided hair. We stood together awkwardly in the dark hallway.

"I'm here to see Miss Crawford," I explained.

"Wait here," she said curtly, ushering me into a lobby-sized living room. A decorator had obviously passed through, but now the rugs and the large upholstered pieces were covered in plastic, undoubtedly to protect them against the activities of two small white poodles that seemed to have the run of the house.

In a few minutes the same woman returned, sans scarf and with some makeup added. The bone structure was there, the outline of the lips was recognizable, but everything else was like a rubbing from an old bas-relief, only suggesting the original art. She led me into the kitchen where she had been using an opened ironing board, and we started the conversation as she moved to the stove and started to prepare a chicken for stewing. There was no household help that I could see.

"I always use Lowry's Seasoned Salt on my chicken," said Joan Crawford, a cooking hint which promptly entered, and remained, in my permanent culinary repertoire.

It was spooky and surreal to watch her rubbing the spice into the chicken with her bare hands, washing them, and then putting away the ironing board. Was this the final grounding of all my fantasies, the end of a journey from then to the present? Inside me, a twelve-year-old wept for the lost world of Joan and Franchot, the inevitable evening chill that overtakes us all.

"Would you like to see the apartment upstairs?" asked Crawford.

"Of course," I responded. We went upstairs, to the bedroom that must have been originally sumptuous but now seemed frowzy and dark. She demonstrated the electric buttons that opened up the heavy draperies and raised and lowered the huge bed.

"Al loved this bed," she said wistfully, patting it with her hand.

Then the mood changed. I followed her into the bathroom-dressing room area. She pushed the switch that turned on the rows of stage light bulbs rimming the mirrored walls, the huge dressing table. In one corner was a ceiling-high crystal étagère, its seven or eight shelves crowded with magnum bottles of perfume, all wearing the most expensive labels. The ostentation was dated, but it resonated with my matinee maven memories.

Then she flung open the doors to a cavernous closet behind the mirrors.

"I designed this myself," she said proudly, and stepped in. There were dozens and dozens of dresses precisely arranged by color: short ones and formal long gowns, with a separate rack for suits and blouses. There were orderly rows of transparent plastic boxes for hats: big-brimmed numbers and pillboxes and evening concoctions. Another bank of boxes contained handbags for which herds of cattle, lizards, and alligators had died. There was also a completely separate closet for what she told was more than 300 pairs of shoes.

This was more like it. The tunnels of time leading back opened and unclogged. It was make-believe time again, and I had stepped into wonderland. Old movies and modern reality melted into one another.

"When I was in high school," I said, and I swear there was a catch in my voice, "I went to my first high school dance in a black dress with big organdy sleeves. It was a knockoff of that gown you wore in *Letty Lynton*."

"Oh yes," said Crawford, giving the line a throaty reading. "Adrian did that for me. It was one of my favorites."

Why is that moment so indelible even now? Because despite all the years of editing and writing, the quest for fresh angles and newsmaking scoops that would sell, I remain an incurable romantic. Yes, I came to realize that all that scintillates is sometimes sleaze, that fame can be and is fabricated by greedy manipulators, that the Beautiful People are all too often users, in every sense of the word. But for better or for worse, I still clap to show my belief in Tinkerbell, and I am still not jaded by star dazzle.

Much later, in 1974, I chose not to publish *Mommie Dearest* in the *Journal* because I thought its portrait of Joan by her daughter was too kinky and too cruel. Its shock value rubbed off on the child as well as the parent. Instead we bought *Joan Crawford* by Bob Thomas, which we subtitled *Dark Side of a Star*. It too chronicled her extremes, her instabilities, her neurotically abusive treatment of her adopted children. But it also paid homage to Joan Crawford the star and the legend, and helped to explain some of the things that made that obsessive, mixed-up lady the strange woman she was in private life . . . the real Joan Crawford, not Faye Dunaway.

Even without market research, I know that magazine readers have always shared my appetite for star dazzle. Most lives do not sparkle; many are filled with monotony and pain. Actors, sports stars, and other celebrities provide an escapist reality that relieves the cramping dailiness of enforced selfhood. And so, at *McCall's* and the *Journal,* I stalked the stars and hunted the headliners—and their flacks stalked and hunted me.

Fortunately, the period predated slightly our current era of total media saturation. The proliferation of TV talk shows, cable interview specials, docu-dramas, "soft news features," gossip tabloids, and such publications as *People* and *US* had not yet formed that huge leeching network that sucks the last bit of detail out of even vivid celebrities and leaves only bloodless, boring clichés. *(Charlie's Angels,* for example, ended up as much victims of its press overkill as of poor scriptwriters.)

Back in those days, we at the women's magazines, with our

devoted following of millions of women, were the big game in town. Every producer, every agent, every publicity person knocked himself or herself out pitching for space. And vying for that pinnacle prize: the cover. Covers. How publicity people and stars themselves used to woo for them! Today, stars and their press agents are more arrogant—demanding cover picture approval, bargaining between magazines for the best deal, refusing to use any photographer but their favorite, and protesting if a desperate editor ends up using a stock shot from a past sitting. (Barbra Streisand was one of the most difficult subjects. My best cover of her was bought without her approval from the photographer who had done one of her record albums.)

But those were different days. And so I was breakfasted, lunched, and dined. I met Judy Garland, Charlton Heston (he brought along his daughter, Holly), John Wayne, Rex Harrison. But never, unfortunately, Garbo. I always wanted to interview this mysterious lady who lived like a recluse in her apartment near the East River. The closest we ever got was an exclusive picture story executive editor John Stevens picked up when he went to Sweden to interview the King. And, of course, Thomas Tryon's *roman à clef* novel *Fedora*, whose heroine was based on Greta Garbo.

Grace Kelly. When she died this past September, I felt as if it were a personal blow. I had met her many times through the years. But I believe I am one of the few who remembers how she *really* met Prince Rainier, although all the obituaries said it was during the filming of *To Catch a Thief.* Actually, their introduction took place as part of a *McCall's* fashion feature in 1954, when we sent her over to model *McCall's* patterns in the Monaco palace gardens with the man whom we had featured as one of the world's most eligible bachelors, Prince Rainier. She acknowledged our role as matchmaker much later, when John Carter and I went down to a party in Philadelphia for the Rainiers' fifth anniversary, a folksy brannigan at the Belle-vue Stratford Hotel, given by the Kelly family's favorite un-dertaker. Princess Grace, looking beautiful and happy, gave full credit to *McCall's* as matchmaker, and remembered the dresses she wore: rose prints. Later, I met Princess Grace in Monaco, and even drove down that dangerous road on which her fatal accident took place.

As movies and movie audiences changed, as TV became more and more important, I started to look for new faces and rising stars. I spent one afternoon with that new comedic kook from Brooklyn, Woody Allen, at the Manhattan brownstone he had bought with his bride, Louise Lasser. We talked of many things, including death, which fit in with the dark de-cor, prophetic of later films like *Interiors*. But it didn't seem to have much to do with *What's New Pussycat?*, the movie I was there to discuss, for which he had written the screenplay, and in which he appeared.

On the other hand, I had a sunny, effervescent breakfast at the Plaza with a sexy starlet for whom the whole world seemed to be opening like a flower. Life proved otherwise. Her name was Sharon Tate.

And then there was actor Ben Gazzara, who never really made it to the summit, but whom I first was intrigued with in the stage production of *A Hatful of Rain*. I guess I became really smitten with Gazzara in the TV series *Run for Your Life,* one of the ever-cloned genre in which a character must move from place to place escaping or searching. In his case he was a man with an unspecified fatal disease. (Its terminal stages turned out to be network cancellation.) Gazzara's sharp-edged acting ability gave depth to the character and made each episode a sexy, dramatic, bittersweet entity, surefire pop drama.

"I know, I know," my husband would say as I went upstairs early every week to turn on the set. "You're running for your weekly fix."

To prove this was all professional interest I arranged to interview Gazzara. At the time, he was married to actress Janice Rule.

We chose the Oak Room at the Plaza as a meeting place, a dark, busy bar that I have always considered one of the most romantic spots in New York. I got there early, and he waved from across the room, and then joined me, making every female head in the room swivel. He turned out to be just as magnetic off-camera as on, and as he ordered up an expensive bottle of Dom Perignon champagne, I asked questions and took notes and felt marvelous. It could have gone on beyond the second bottle of Dom Perignon, but he had a theater date and had to leave. Three women rushed out into the hall to catch me at the checkroom.

"Is he really as great as he seems to be?" they asked me. I assured them, from the breadth of my two-hour exposure, that he was.

That weekend, I was visiting a neighbor in Riverdale who wanted me to meet a young friend of hers, married to an art director at *Good Housekeeping*. We chatted about women's magazines and their fringe benefits, and I related the details of my encounter with Gazzara. I noticed that she was smiling peculiarly.

"You've met him?" I asked.

"Sort of," she responded. "I was once married to him." I looked at her unbelievingly. There had been nothing in the bio about this.

"Very briefly," she explained. "He was just a young actor starting in New York. I was a kid, too."

"Is he really as great as he seems?" I echoed, keyhole-peeking journalist mixed with curious fan.

She laughed.

"He is an *actor*," she said discreetly. "Keep your illusions and don't spoil them." And we dropped it at that, although when I got home, I could have kicked myself.

Two of my other "discoveries" did hit the jackpot. Once PR man Vic Ghidalia urged me to come up and meet one of their new ABC-TV stars who was making his debut that season in *Hawk,* a detective series about an Iroquois police lieutenant named John Hawk.

I watched them shooting a scene, and then they brought over the tall, dark leading man with the great build and the ultra-bright smile. We drew up camp chairs and, considering the fact that I was probably one in a long chain of interviews, he was cordial, funny, and full of good quotes.

"You look slightly Indian," I said. "Do you have any Indian blood?"

"I'm part Cherokee," he said, "and I'm glad you asked. I'm hoping this show can do for Indians what Cosby did for blacks, break down the stereotypes." That was before he started to collect all those scalps: Judy, Dinah, Tammy, Chris, Sally, Loni, and the rest of the squaws. His name: Burt Reynolds.

Another star I met early was Robert Redford, whose performance with Barbra Streisand in *The Way We Were* still ranks as my No. 1 movie turn-on. (And pooh to Pauline Kael, who called him "overripe.")

I first met Redford in 1965. He had just finished the role of the homosexual actor in *Inside Daisy Clover,* a rather daring part for a starting performer to take on. The star was Natalie Wood, and I was told I could interview her if I would also separately spend some time with a new guy named Robert Redford. What could I lose?

It was not exactly an effervescent interview. He came on as shy and self-conscious. But he was intelligent, and he seemed to take the world and his craft very seriously. I predicted to him (and to myself) that he was going to go far. ("Now when do I get Natalie Wood?" I asked the press agent in the hall.)

I followed Redford's career in *The Chase* and *This Property Is Condemned*, and after *Butch Cassidy and the Sundance Kid*, I knew he'd never be a publicity trade-off again, and I wrote him a sincere congratulatory personal note.

One day, I was visiting Harvard University with my husband and daughter, and as we were walking through an underground shopping center, we bumped into a young couple casually dressed in ski clothes. The man was unshaven. "Lenore, what are you doing here?" He laughed, and thanked me for my letter. I introduced them—Bob and Lola Redford—to my husband and Jane, who was about sixteen at the time.

"Who was that?" asked Jane, who had not been paying much attention, and was anxious to get into one of the college boutiques.

"That was Robert Redford." Her response was very rhinestony.

Interviews with the elusive Redford were difficult to get. We once ran a dialogue between him and Ralph Nader, which nobody read. In October 1980, we used Redford as the first male to be featured alone on our cover (we tested it first) and the issue sold like hotcakes. We photographed him in a ski sweater, for which we craftily offered knitting instructions. Inside, we showed a shot of him in rimless wire glasses, with the gray clearly salting his strawberry blond sideburns. He spoke of how his kids sing a ditty to him: "R.R. Superstar, who the hell do you think you are?" He broke through the usual wall of privacy to discuss his twenty-one-year marriage. "The secret of a good marriage is change. It's gotta move, if it stops, it's dead." But he grew defiantly resistant when asked how he handled the temptation of other women. "That's my business," he answered.

120

The article *was* good for his business, which at that point happened to be his production of *Ordinary People*. But I hear that he was disturbed by the intimacy of the piece, although he did not send us one of the long critical letters he has been known to dispatch when an article offends his sense of what is right and proper to say about him. So many contemporary stars want it all ways: the fame and the privacy, their own convictions and the adoration of the masses, who prefer opinionless heroes and heroines. I respect and admire Robert Redford. And I think performers do have the right to speak out and work for what they believe. But, like the masses, I most cherish the way R.R. was in *The Way We Were*.

As for Natalie Wood, I did get to see her several times, too, in both of her marriages to Robert Wagner. I particularly recall one golden afternoon with her in her Hollywood home, a meeting that I remembered with particular poignancy after her tragic death.

Celebrities were beginning to come out of the new music world. In a visit to London, I heard about a new group called The Beatles, and I got myself an interview with Brian Epstein. One day in 1970, I decided to prevail on John Lennon, who had already written a book of poetry, to write a special poem on commission for *McCall's*. (My daughter Jane and her friend Debby stole his phone number from a memo pad and flashed it around school.)

He sent it in. Much later, after his death, I arranged to have a copy of it sent to Yoko Ono for their son.

Called "The Toy Boy," it was a long, rambling, somewhat obfuscated verse about a small boy's Christmas toys as they talked about their sleeping master. One verse sticks in my mind.

> The Clock struck eight, as clocks will do.
> At eight o'clock—that's nothing new

Except that this clock never could.
The clock obligingly conferred,
"I will not chime unless I'm heard!"
He was an artiste, so you see—
He didn't like to chime for free!
You know how it is.*

John Lennon didn't chime for free, either. He charged us a hefty fee which, I recall, Bob Stein thought was excessive for a poem he suspected had shadowy not-so-childish meanings.

There was also a fun lunch at the Four Seasons with a young duo out of Forest Hills who were about to give their first big concert at Lincoln Center. Their names were Paul Simon and Art Garfunkel, and we hit it off immediately. Jane was home with a bad cold, so I called for a table telephone and told her I had two friends who wanted to say hello. It was better medicine than antibiotics.

S&G sent me good seats to the concert, and I sat right behind Paul Simon's mother. I congratulated her, and she wistfully complained that she had not been allowed to go backstage to see her son.

Like a bridge over troubled waters, I gave her my business card and suggested that she try again, identifying herself as me. It worked, proving that the press is more powerful than motherhood.

But the one star who fascinated me the most—and incidentally produced the best copy and cover lines—was always Richard Burton.

I quote from my own by-lined article in the January 1965 *McCall's*.

An interview with Richard Burton is, to put it mildly,

---

*Copyright © 1965 by John Lennon.

122

an experience. He talks with an effortless eloquence and erudition that outpaces even shorthand notes. He is not good-looking in the matinee-idol sense: but his granite features are lighted with a bonfire of human warmth and sensitivity underneath. He is as complex as a crystal: one moment crude and earthy, another soaring into lofty literary language. But he is always dazzling.

I had wanted to do my big take-out on Burton ever since the first night I met him. That was when he just finished playing King Arthur in the Broadway musical *Camelot* and he was on his way to join the cast of *Cleopatra*. PR man Ned McDavid invited me to one of those lavish exploitation parties which are given to garner air time and ink. In this case, the Chrysler Company was exploiting its upcoming TV special which featured Maurice Chevalier, Richard Burton, and Robert Goulet among others, and all were on board to greet the press at the relocated El Morocco, the former society nightclub with the famous zebra banquettes.

It was a good party and I stayed late. Toward the end, a group of us, including Richard Burton, crowded into a small elevator that took you from the main room at street level. The elevator balked for about ten minutes, and amidst the crush of inebriated bodies, the ribald repartee flew. Burton gave us all a funny account of his only previous meeting with Elizabeth, whom he had stepped on beside a swimming pool in Hollywood. (Later stories surfaced that she had known him for years as a friend, which I doubt.) He described the top of her torso in hearty hyperbole, and then shouted across the jammed elevator:

"You can tell that ——— Harrison to move over. Mark Antony's on his way." Taylor, who was already established in Rome with her present husband, Eddie Fisher, plus three children from previous marriages, was recovering from her latest round of serious illnesses. Just before the Christmas holidays, she was having trouble with her leg, and there was more pessimistic talk about her canceling out. In January 1962, Burton and Taylor played their first scene together, and thus began what was then called "the most public adultery in the world."

Burton's wife of almost thirteen years, Sybil, went to New York, where I also interviewed her. A Welsh actress with prematurely silver hair and a fast, literate tongue, she did not seem insecure when I spent the afternoon in her Central Park West apartment. At that time, friends were holding fast to their view that even Taylor was no match for the loving Sybil, who was always willing to welcome Burton back from his many flings. I could understand this feeling. Sybil was warm, witty, compassionate, speaking of her husband with both understanding and tough irony. Their older daughter, Kate, who at twenty-four received a degree from the Yale Drama School and today is acting professionally, was off at primary school. But the younger child, Jessica, who must have been about three at the time, wandered in and out. She did not speak, but pulled at her mother's dress and at objects on the coffee table. At one point, when Sybil was out of the room, I amused the pretty child by drawing crayon pictures for her.

"Usually, Jessica doesn't take to strangers," said Sybil. This of course was the Burton daughter later diagnosed as autistic, and who has been institutionalized for most of her life.

At the time, the press covered the fact that Richard's foster-father, Philip, was standing by Sybil, and had sent Burton a cablegram in Rome critical of his involvement with Elizabeth. Burton, furious, telephoned Philip, and the ensuing estrangement lasted for two years.

I scented a story there, so through publicist John Springer, and with Sybil's backup, I got in touch with Philip Burton at his Chelsea apartment. Thus began one of my more intriguing relationships, which I wrote up in *McCall's* in an article titled "The Other Burton."

Philip Burton was sixty then, a gentle drama coach and Shakespearean expert who was teaching in New York at the American Musical and Dramatic Academy. He agreed to work with me on an in-depth story on Richard, and through the older man, I got a perceptive and unique fix on the incredible young Welshman who was taking the world by storm—especially since he joined forces with Elizabeth.

Richard Burton was born Richard Walter Jenkins on November 10, 1925, in Pontrhydfen, Wales, the twelfth son in a mining family of thirteen. His mother died early, and his natural father, a tippling cock-sparrow of a man, was obviously a character who could handle a strong draft of rhetoric as well as of beer. After his mother's death, Richard lived chiefly with his sister Cecelia; he claimed that many of Elizabeth's qualities reminded him of "Sis."

Meanwhile, Philip Burton was teaching at the nearby Port Talbot grammar school. Son of an Englishman who had gone to Wales to work in the mines and had died in a pit rock-slide, Philip found his vocation in playing Pygmalion to young students with a flair for theater. "Wild Jenk" caught his attention: "He always had a natural flair for poetry," and despite some voice problems, Philip Burton coached him into a discernible acting talent.

"It was a common practice in Wales for benefactors to help worthy boys and girls," Sybil told me. Because there was just short of twenty-one years' difference in their ages, Philip could not procure regular adoption papers, but in 1943 Richard became Philip's ward and took his name. It was Philip who cast him in amateur productions, then recommended him for an audition with actor Emlyn Williams. The relationship between Philip and Richard remained strong through the years, until the incident in which Philip sided with Sybil and Richard fumed.

But the tie was picked up just before Burton and Taylor married. Richard Burton was rehearsing *Hamlet* in Toronto. Uneasy after a long absence from the stage and a heavy diet of screaming headlines, he was in trouble and needed Philip.

One day from her hotel suite in Toronto, Elizabeth herself called the man she had never met and pleaded, "Please, he needs you." Philip would not go without checking with Sybil. She looked at him with large soft eyes, so much like her rival's, and said, "Go, he needs you."

Philip went to Canada, patched up the rift, and helped Richard to get his act together. On his return, we spent a lot of time together.

Hamlet in Toronto was an audience success but a critical failure. From there it went to Boston, where mobs manhandled the newlyweds, and then it came to New York. Which is where my professional involvement paid off. I was put right in the middle of the tumult that occurred every day and night at the Lunt-Fontanne Theater, where *Hamlet* was playing to packed houses, and where Liz and Richard will return this spring in *Private Lives*. The crowds swirled around the corner of Broadway and Forty-sixth Street: squads of mounted police with clubs kept the frenzied fans behind barriers. It was a seventeen-week run of what *Variety* called the highest-grossing, most profitable Shakespeare production in history. Liz defined her husband as "the Frank Sinatra of Shakespeare."

And thanks to Philip, I got involved in it all. I saw *Hamlet* with him three times. The first time, the whole audience had to leave because of a bomb scare. The second time, Philip annotated every scene for me. "See that bit of business there. He's putting on four extra minutes because I'm in the house!" The third time was a more strained performance because

Richard had just returned after a cancellation of shows due to pain from some bone changes in his cervical spine. On each of my visits I went backstage, where the Burton dressing room was full of hubbub and glamour and guests like Mike Nichols and Gloria Steinem, who were dating at the time.

I had talked to Richard a few times alone, but I wanted to catch him with Elizabeth in a double interview about Philip. So, the third evening, we arranged to have a post-show dinner at Jim Downey's restaurant, where Elizabeth would meet us.

"Tell you what, luv," said Richard, putting his arm around me. "You walk out ahead of me to the car. Pull that coat of yours over your head and see what it feels like to have the pack after you."

So I learned about star frazzle. It was fabulous, but frightening. The squealing hordes trying to get to the chauffeured Rolls-Royce. (One woman actually *kissed* the car.) The pushing and shoving, the shouts of "Let's see your face, Liz" and one disappointed cry of "Oh, it's not *her!*" If all this wasn't enough of a trauma, I got myself into a contretemps inside the car with Richard, who was still talking about his spinal problems. I had discussed them that morning with my husband, who had given me his medical opinion that Burton's pain was a fairly common condition, and that he would undoubtedly recover.

In an effort to be consoling, I repeated this, using the phrase "fairly common condition." Burton froze and would not speak to me until we got to the restaurant, where Philip took me aside and explained that Richard had much guilt about walking off the stage in pain and would not want the cause to be "fairly common." I shrugged, decided that apologies would only make things worse, and went back to the table to join him and Elizabeth. She looked beautiful as ever, ate heartily, and except for teasing him once in a while, was every inch the supportive wife. It turned out to be a warm and memorable evening, with Burton at his best remembering anecdotes about his childhood.

Burton's mercurial sensitivity, like his eternal love affair with alcohol, was well known. It was further documented much later, when with John Springer and John Carter, I went down to visit Elizabeth Taylor—then Mrs. John Warner—in their gracious Washington home. We were there on a secret project: The three of us had joined in a short-lived TV production company to put Taylor into a series casting her as the editor of a women's magazine. She didn't want to go back to work at the time. Later, she opted for the stage and *The Little Foxes*. And the house has been sold.

Somehow the conversation got around to tempers, and looking around to make sure husband John wasn't in the room, she asked John Springer: "Remember the night Richard kicked the television set?" Giggling, she recalled it for us.

The Burtons had been staying at the Regency Hotel during the *Hamlet* engagement, and Elizabeth had stayed home with a cold. There was an old Peter Sellers movie on the tube, and she was watching it when Richard came home.

He sat down next to her on the sofa and moaned.

"They booed me tonight," he said. "For the first time in my life I was booed."

Elizabeth stroked him absently and said, "I'm sure there was nothing to it. Let me watch Peter's last scene, and we'll talk about it."

Richard howled, got up, and walked over to the TV set.

"I get booed and you have to watch this ——— movie?" he shouted. And he put his foot through the TV screen, shattering the glass.

Pandemonium prevailed. His foot began to bleed, no minor matter for a man with a chronic disposition to hemophilia. Elizabeth had to find a doctor, the leg was treated, and Richard almost had to cancel another night's performance.

I must admit, she told the story with relish, and then looked over her shoulder to make sure that John Warner wasn't in the hall listening. That day, I also remember being impressed with the fortune in French Impressionists she had hanging on her walls . . . including a magnificent Renoir.

"I started investing in these early," she said. "Remember that my parents ran an art gallery and my uncle, Howard Young, was a big dealer in New York. I have been a collector all my life. One of my better moves."

Elizabeth Taylor. I guess I have worked on more stories on her and ran more magazine covers on her than on any other star in the business. Each marriage of the seven (two were to Burton, of course) was cause for another story. It is hard to realize she is over fifty now, and the blurb on Kitty Kelley's book *Elizabeth Taylor: The Last Star* sums it up well.

"Again and again she has bounced back from illnesses and disasters that seemed impossible to surmount, packing into one lifetime more glamour, controversy, more romance than any other woman in this century—perhaps in *any* century—perhaps to emerge as the ultimate star."

We bought the Kitty Kelley book for $99,000 to run in three parts in the *Journal,* the last major book purchased before I left the editorship. Kitty and I talked while she was working on it, and she credits me in her acknowledgments. I put her on to some sources, reminded her of some published articles, and urged her to not let it slip into a mere rip-and-hack job. Taylor is easy to target. The pageant of her life is filled with flamboyancy and folly, and today she is especially open to caricature. But she does have redeeming qualities, and she is a landmark. The Kelley book turned out to be a spicy but well-rounded portrait, and despite objections from some of Taylor's intimates, it deserved to be a best seller. (There was one story cut by the publishers from the book. It was about an abortion she was rumored to have had after an early love affair with a famous performer.)

Richard Burton was a writer as well as an actor, turning out prose as articulate and literary as his conversation. While he was in Sicily filming a rather negligible movie in 1974 called *The Voyage,* with Sophia Loren, we asked him to do a piece about his co-star. (He was then estranged from Elizabeth.) The piece was written on location, on his yacht, on the jet that took him back to California for a reunion with his wife, and finally completed in Naples and Venice. I loved his description of Sophia: "Great cook, great cook . . . Cold as gold sometimes. Warm as toast other times . . . Survivor. Outlive us all, including our children." And his closing lines: "Night coming down in Venice. Having spent all night in bed with Elizabeth for real and all day with Sophia for unreal. Not bad when you've come from the bowels of the earth."

Sophia. Another sturdy classic proving that Socrates was wrong when he said "Beauty is a short-lived reign." Over two decades, whenever a strong, delineated magazine cover model was needed, chestnut-tressed and recognizable, you reached once more for Sophia, those high cheekbones sometimes even more haunting under the circle of a big hat. In 1968, I interviewed her on the phone in Italy as she took to her bed to ensure the arrival of Carlo Ponti, Jr. ("Cipi"), later to be followed by a second son, Edoardo. In January 1971 it was time to roll out another profile, and I decided to write it myself. First I joined her at the photographer's studio with a lot of fashions to wear, and she handed me two fistfuls of jewels to hold, including an emerald ring slightly smaller than an ice rink. (A few days later, it was part of a half-million-dollar haul by some jewel thieves who seized the gems from the spunky Sophia only by implicitly threatening Cipi's life.) Later, at her apartment, I spent three more hours collecting those pleasant, pithy quotes Sophia usually has on tap about

My favorite talking head, Merv—he brought out the ham in me.
Photograph by Ken Abbinante.

Photography session with the Fords in Vail. We were about to run Betty's book in the *Journal*. *Photograph by Charles W. Bush/Charles Bush Photographers.*

Even off the slopes, Jean-Claude Killy was gorgeous. *Photograph by Burns Photography.*

My Rose period—a tough and re-markable woman. *Photograph by Guy Gillette.*

The Duke didn't need a nametag. *Photograph by Jay Seymour/*
Werner J. Kuhn.

Champions at any age—Forest Hills stars Chris Evert and Hazel Hotchkiss Wightman. *Photograph by Jay Seymour/Werner J. Kuhn.*

Truman Capote: talented, charming, and wicked. *Photograph by Jerry Abramowitz.*

Jacqueline Susann. The critics didn't like her, but readers loved her and friends cherished her. *Photograph by Jay Seymour/Werner J. Kuhn.*

Liz Carpenter, Betty Friedan, and Sey Chassler of *Redbook*, at the Houston Women's Conference Torch Relay. *Photograph by Ann Chwatsky.*

life, love, sex, women, and marriage. She is always a feast for the eyes; always gracious; so gut-physical one wonders why her much older producer-husband, Carlo Ponti, would ever use his noted wandering eye. Sophia Loren hasn't had a real movie hit in ages; it took her imprisonment in Italy to stir up some press excitement for her again. Maybe her problem is that underneath it all, she is what she seems to be, a ripe woman who specializes in womanliness—and time has moved on to other styles. Except in perfume: her name seems to work for a popular fragrance line.

Gina Lollobrigida was a different dish of pasta.

Kathy Berlin of Rogers and Cowan, one of the most competent and best-liked publicists in town (she's married to NBC correspondent Richard Valeriani), brought Gina to the *Journal* in 1974 in connection with *My Italy,* a new book of photographs she had just brought out. Gina, the prototype old-fashioned sex goddess, arrived at the office in a leopard hat and skirt, weighted down by the cameras she had now adopted as her second career. Even with discernible laugh lines on her face, and a few extra pounds padding those voluptuous curves, she still caused ripples as she took over the office, dropping world-famous names like rose petals and proudly showing us hundreds of her prints. Cartier-Bresson she wasn't, but you could at least identify who her subjects were. It gave us an idea.

We started to negotiate on a series to be called "The World's Most Interesting Men," in which Gina would be named our editor-at-large. (I figured it was worth it just to bring her to our next *Journal* advertising sales meeting.) We decided to start at the top. Our new Secretary of State, Henry Kissinger, seemed like a good prospect. He had recently abandoned his "swinger" reputation to woo tall, intelligent Nancy Maginnes, but they never seemed to be in the same place long enough to get married. Would he grant a sitting (or reclining?) to Gina Lollobrigida? He certainly would. We had to cable Gina in Australia, where she was photographing teeny-bopper idol David Cassidy, to get her home in time for the appointment in Washington on March 20.

Photographer and subject got along swimmingly. He saw her alone, and closed the door of his apartment while she worked. They had dinner in the State Department dining room. He gave her nice quotes and an even nicer invitation to join him in Acapulco for the Easter holidays, when he expected to return home from a Russian trip.

There turned out to be some loopholes in the linguini. First of all, her business demands were wild. She asked a ridiculous fee for becoming an editor-at-large. Her expense accounts were staggering; she would stay only at the Waldorf-Astoria, and required a limousine to take her the few blocks from there to the office. She also tried to charge us for some expensive books she had bought. I started to get cold feet about the whole deal, although executive editor Dick Kaplan was eager to travel with her and Kathy Berlin on an upcoming trip to Cuba to visit Fidel Castro. (I stopped that hijack.) She had already lined up astronaut Neil Armstrong as a subject, but mostly, we all were dying to find out what would happen to Gina and Henry in Mexico.

One day in March, our articles editor, Mary Fiore, who lived in the same apartment house as Nancy Maginnes, came in with a flash bulletin.

"I think Nancy's going to marry Henry the K," she said. "I saw her in the laundry last night putting her beach clothes and summer cottons in the machine."

Mary was right. Kissinger and Nancy Maginnes were married on March 30, and flew off to Acapulco in one of Rockefeller's private jets. There was no need to drag things out with Gina. We assigned Marvin Kalb to do a story on the new Mrs. Kissinger, with a male photographer, and said *arrivederci* to

Gina. It wasn't all that easy; she brought her lawyers in and we had to pay a hefty settlement. Gina is still photographing, and even came back to make peace with a new editor at the *Journal*. I bet Gina would have loved to have her camera handy the day that female nuke nut was throttled by Nancy (for saying Kissinger liked *boys?*) in the airport.

SEVEN

Re: Lax and Other Outposts

Editors-in-chief should not take days off. It is the Hershey corollary to Murphy's law: "Anything that can go wrong, will." Add: "Especially if you've gone out of town." Bad or good, you will not be there to see it happen.

A spy on your staff will find out that the lead story in your competitor's magazine is almost identical to yours, with three great quotes your writer didn't get. Your production editor will find a famous name misspelled on the already engraved cover. There will be a hallway argument between the temperamental fashion editor and the irritable beauty editor. A company memo will announce a shift in management duties. The chairman of the board will call from Tokyo and leave no message. You will miss the birth of a good friend's baby, another friend will need you desperately to save her crumbling marriage, and there will be a never-again one-day towel sale at Bloomingdale's. Your art director's puppy will chew up an irreplaceable transparency. Wherever you have gone, there will be pouring rain. All in all, you will regret leaving.

Editing is a job for workaholics, non-clockwatchers whose noses are comfortable only up against the grindstone. Except that the view from the grindstone is limiting. Editors who are

135

too cloistered, who see only people with similar interests, and regard west of the Hudson as "out there," become provincial in their perspective, New York City hicks.

Despite my only partially conquered fear of flying, I have always managed to cut it both ways. Home base has never been neglected. I keep in telephone touch with a frequency on which AT&T must have based their advertising campaign— not to mention last year's profit statement.

But I have also covered the country, meeting resources and readers, finding out what they like to read in Richmond, what's doing in Denver, which ideas are brewing in Berkeley. Sometimes, my husband's commitments and my own mesh conveniently. Thus, alone or with him, I have been in each of the fifty states except South Carolina, Utah, and Wyoming. Flights have ranged from routine to hair-raising. Another Hershey law: "If you are late or limping, the plane is always at the furthest gate."

The white-knuckle flights are best forgotten.

But one trip worth recalling was the "red-eye" overnight trip from San Francisco to New York, as I rushed home to become editor-in-chief of the *Journal* the next morning.

Alone, tired, tense, I was looking forward to some diverting conversation to get my mind off the situation. My seatmate proved to be a silent businesslike type who extracted dark eyeshades from his briefcase, plugged in the headphones between the seats, and conked out. Across the aisle, a young couple in jeans barely awaited the dimming of the lights to make a tent of their blanket and establish their credentials in the Mile High Club. Cut off from human contact, I spent the first three hours staring out of the darkened plane at the moonlit dark carpet unrolling beneath me, pierced with concentrated pinpoints of light as we passed over city after city.

For comfort, I tried to picture the people behind the lights: insomniacs, late-night workers, mothers tending sick children, guests who refused to go home, and worriers pacing the floor pondering what the *Journal* was going to be like for the next couple of years under its new editor.

I joined them in their contemplation. I had been indoctrinated in all the media gobbledegook: market positioning, demographics, strategies for advance planning. To me, it all boiled down to creating a magazine that had its own recognizable personality and its own function—most of all, a magazine that made a warm connection with women of all ages (although our target has traditionally been women in their thirties). I knew the country spread out beneath me was filled with regional and sectional differences, but there were strong commonalities, too. I believed women wanted help with their daily lives, but something more, too. Involvement, inspiration, a zest and joy for living. Scribbling on the back of an envelope (like Lincoln) I started to jot down ideas, including an article about women who are lonely at the top, particularly at 38,000 feet. I finally relaxed, rang for the flight attendant and ordered a Scotch. I woke up just before we landed at Kennedy.

Since that time I have crisscrossed the country, with and without our publisher, our ad director and other editors, gathering in the sheaves and sowing the word. I have spoken before women's groups and college audiences, which I particularly enjoy. I have also made my share of radio and TV appearances.

When I first took over as chief editor, the ad director and publisher wanted to go to Detroit to convince automobile manufacturers to invest more money in the women's market, as yet unrecognized. My business cohorts felt I should not come along.

"It's a man's town," they explained.

"If you don't have the guts to take along your woman editor, you don't deserve the business," I exploded.

They were shamed into taking me, and I decided to knock them out of their socks.

Promotion director Pat Kyle, research genius Mary Powers, and I put together a smashing presentation proving how women, both working women and homemakers, were already showing their power at the dealer level, and we made the round of ad agencies. I called Dollie Cole, the dynamic wife of Ed Cole, then president of General Motors, whom I had met on a previous visit. When I repeated that "man's town" bit to her, she laughed and said, "We'll show 'em." Dolly arranged a high-powered dinner in my honor at the posh Detroit Athletic Club, and turned out the presidents of all the major companies, and their wives. Not only did I glimpse my guys separating from their socks, but we also got the business, and I think made a breakthrough for a lot of other women's magazines as well.

"I love New York." The song is no phony: Most of us battered, buffeted, but bewitched New Yorkers do. We grumble and complain about the grittiness and the gridlock. But no other place has its infinite variety, its density of seekers and strivers looking for fame, success, and love. It is the communications hub of the world, with people who enjoy the creation of books, magazines, and newspapers, and others who read them with addictive pleasure. It is a woman's city, filled with glorious shopping. It has countless cuisines, from epicurean restaurants to down-to-earth delis. It jostles, it hustles, it sometimes cruelly destroys. But it is a city that is ennui-proof. I love New York and proudly wear the Big Apple pin that Lew Rudin, real estate mogul and civic leader, gives to many of its lovers. But that doesn't mean that I can't crowd a few more cities into my affections too.

For example, I love San Francisco. Its *joie de vivre* is more quirky, but those views and the food and its well-dressed sophistication are irresistible. I love Boston for its civilized air of academe and its patina of American history. I love Dallas and Houston because they're rich and self-satisfied and always changing, the essence of Texas. I love the zoo in San Diego, the Garden District of New Orleans, Philadelphia's Society Hill. I love Jacksonville's southern hospitality, Honolulu's caressing climate, like being swathed in velvet, Atlanta's peaches-and-chromium contrasts. Chicago is an hour behind New York, but it's cleaner, lustier, and somehow more mainstream American, whatever that is.

Los Angeles is a special case. Its reputation precedes it: a city of sham and scam, obsessed by money and sex and power. It is the home of hot tubs and air-conditioned hearts. The smog is a plague to sinuses. Without a car, a trip downtown might as well be across the Gobi desert. But when the airport porter puts that baggage tag marked LAX on my luggage, I get anticipatory goose bumps. No matter how ragged or frayed I am, I know I'm in for some bigtime funtime in Tinsel City.

In the many times I've been there, I've occasionally stayed at "the pink palace," the fabled Beverly Hills Hotel, where people tip the bellhop to have their name paged at the pool, and where the Polo Lounge is the place to have lunch if you want to overhear conversations about zillion-dollar TV or movie deals. Once, I even shared a bungalow.

I much prefer the more gracious Beverly Wilshire, within walking distance of Bonwit's and Magnin's and Rodeo Drive. Here, the rooms are elegantly appointed (some even have Jacuzzis), the telephone message system is impeccable, and Helen Chaplin and owner Hernando Courtwright treat me like a press princess. What's more, in the alleyway between the old wing and the new wing, you can watch the most expensive cars this side of a James Bond novel come and go. The Bel Air is even more "in," but I'd rather visit there than stay.

139

I have made at least one or two trips to L.A. each year for the past two decades. Back in the more halcyon days, studios and press agents had unlimited expense accounts. "You look laid out," said a friend of mine, viewing my room crowded with more than fifteen huge, lavish floral arrangements, including an entire orchid plant.

The purpose of my trips was mostly to scout upcoming productions and talk to stars. I did both. My daily calendar was covered with names: Jack Lemmon, Rosalind Russell, Sammy Davis, Jr., Rex Harrison, Mitzi Gaynor, and scores of others. Some of my best interviews were at the performers' homes. It was interesting to see their taste and lifestyles, as interpreted by themselves and by their decorators.

And sometimes I just had a quick coffee or a drink. As I did with comedian Carl Reiner, downstairs at the Wilshire. We discovered to our delight that we had both attended Evander Childs High School in the Bronx, and shared the same French teacher, Mr. Pred. Breaking away reluctantly from Reiner's nonstop wit, I went on to meet my next date, actor Richard Harris, who was waiting for me in front of the hotel in a big white convertible.

Impressively, we started to roll away. A figure jumped off the sidewalk and began waving his arms in the middle of the street. Richard Harris jammed on the brakes, all traffic behind us screeched to a halt, and the horns started to blare. Carl Reiner, doing a cheerleader number, sang:

Fight for Evander, Evander must win,
Fight to the finish, never give in . . .

Harris, a mad-dog Englishman himself, couldn't make head or tail of the shenanigans.

Another time, press representative William Faith picked me up to take me over to the Moorepark Avenue home of his boss, Bob Hope; I felt as if I should change my name to Charity.

It turned out to be a unique afternoon.

Hope's house was traditional, impressive, though not to be compared to the magnificent modern fortress he's more recently built in Palm Springs, which will become a museum when he dies. Bob showed me his putting green, on which a big shag rug was drying. ("The dogs got at it," he said apologetically.) Then we went into his dining room, where we sat and talked about his peripatetic adventures. I thought he ought to write a book about his USO tours, a suggestion he later followed.

"Tell me about your childhood," I said, now that we were comfy. We were off. Bob, of course, is a multi-multi-multi-millionaire, largely thanks to astute real estate investments, but he cannot forget his meager beginnings. At the age of four, Leslie Townes Hope was taken from England by his stonecutter father and mother—the year was 1908—and brought to Cleveland, where he was part of a large, struggling family. At the time of my visit, he was still recovering from the loss of his closest brother, Jack, and this probably was what made him additionally wistful.

"Come on upstairs," he said suddenly. So Faith, Hope, and Hershey climbed the stairs, up past the study in which hundreds of photographs with presidents and politicos and military noncoms were hanging, into the bedroom. Here, like Crawford, he opened a huge clothes closet—except that his seemed to contain enough assorted golf sweaters to equip every pro shop in the United States.

He climbed up on a chair and reached behind his golf hats to a shoebox on the top shelf, held fast with rubber bands.

We pored over the pictures together, the three of us sitting on the bed. At one point, when he was describing each of his six brothers, he actually began to weep. It was painful to both Bill and myself, because the sorrow was obviously nothing so

141

simple that he could be comforted. Finally, he blew his nose and put the pictures away.

"I've never seen anything like it," said Bill Faith on the way home. (He recently has written a fine biography of Hope.) "You must have touched a nerve. Bob usually is a much more guarded man."

I also made the party rounds. Hollywood parties are not different from lavish parties anywhere; they just have more stellar casts. Depending on the host or hostess, the food can be ordinary or palate-tingling. I remember when the former Mrs. Vincente Minnelli (now Denise Hale) started a whole trend by serving baked potatoes stuffed with caviar as a first course. Danny Kaye, of course, loved to cook up his own Chinese food for intimate groups. The town's caterers can go Mexican, Mideastern, Italian, Spanish, or Zen at a telephone call, and outside Manhattan's East Side, there are probably more filet mignons per foot than any other place in the United States.

I went to many of the best socials, largely thanks to the efforts of Vernon Scott, our knowing Hollywood correspondent, who is married to beautiful Jane Wooster Scott. Jane started to paint as a hobby. Today she is one of the nation's best-known primitive painters, and her works are owned by many top collectors, including the most art-conscious movie stars.

I never did attend a full-scale Hollywood debauch, although I have certainly heard reports about them. There was one luau at Rock Hudson's house that gave me a rough idea. Eddie Fisher, Connie Stevens, Barbra Streisand, and crowds of other bankables were drinking and dancing and smoking it up in the torch-lit garden. We left early, and someone asked us to help Phil Silvers find his car, which he had parked in a driveway at the bottom of the hill. Sol and I drove him around from driveway to driveway. Phil, who was tight and having eye problems, said, "There it is. I left the keys in the dash." The next morning, Phil was almost picked up for car theft.

Every year, Vernon and Jane Scott gave a big party in my honor. Drawn as much by Vernon's clout as mine, haute Hollywood turned out in force. Guest lists over the years included the likes of Gregory Peck, Liza Minnelli, Carroll O'Connor, Jonathan Winters, Jerry Lewis, Eva Gabor, Loni Anderson, Jim Nabors, Sidney Sheldon, Deborah Raffin and husband Michael Viner, Mike Connors, Britt Eklund, and so on. One night George Peppard arrived at the Scotts' with three Hollywood hookers in tow. I thought they were just hungry young actresses—Jane always serves marvelous food. But they were identified by some of their recent clients. Peppard, who was once stormily married to Elizabeth Ashley, recently endeared himself to the film community. He was one of the most faithful visitors to the ailing Henry Fonda, dropping in almost every day. In the last weeks, he even forced Hank Fonda into reading aloud from a book of verse, a little each day, until that familiar voice strengthened and returned, giving the actor a sense of normalcy in those final hours.

Friends have always ribbed me about the Hollywood high life, asking me to reveal my own temptations and escapades. Even if I had them, I'd never own up. But I can admit that once I did pick up a seeming admirer, however unlikely. It was Mr. Clean himself, Walt Disney.

The date was late in 1964. Disney, who had just made *Mary Poppins,* was interested in granting an interview with what seemed like a wholesome columnist from a sensible women's magazine.

Again, I was escorted by his press representative, whose name my mind has conveniently erased. All the way to the Disney studios in his car, the flabby flack shared his social and political views with me. He reported how his boss was vigorously working for Goldwater against Johnson in the upcoming election. He made his own insinuating remarks about the religious and racial composition of the movie industry, completely disregarding the possibility that I might violently disagree with him.

"Wait and see the surprise you are going to get when you see Walt's office," he gushed. I could hardly wait. Perhaps I wasn't going to meet Disney at all; there would be instead an Animatronic figure of himself, programmed like the Abraham Lincoln model at the World's Fair. But Walt Disney was the real thing, an affable man in an ordinary office. I thought I had missed something.

The press agent made it perfectly clear.

"Didn't you notice?" he exclaimed. "He had a *colored* secretary!" By colored, he meant black, and I had not noticed. I couldn't wait to get back to my hotel. This horrid man didn't deserve a berth in the same barn with The Three Little Pigs.

The Disney interview was fascinating. Walt Disney spent almost all morning sharing his convictions about the entertainment business, the nation, and the world. Mostly, he concentrated on his feelings about the movie business, which he felt was doomed to disaster if it continued its trend of producing depressing, dirty movies that were not fit for American families. He could not then predict that the industry would change audiences.

He told me that the night before he had screened *Days of Wine and Roses* in his own home, and he could not bear to watch it until the end.

"Who needs that kind of morbid story?" he asked. "Audiences want to be uplifted, not taken down into the gutter in the name of arty nonsense." There was a rim of hysteria to his voice as he asked: "Did *you* see that picture? Did *you* like it?" Fortunately, I had not caught up with it as yet. When I did,

144

the following week, I thought it was disturbing but powerful, with great performances by Jack Lemmon and Lee Remick.

Disney was pleased by my seeming agreement, mostly conveyed by punctuating nods and weak smiles. He asked me about myself, how I had become an editor, where I lived, where I worked, how much time I spent with my daughter. (His two daughters were grown.) There was something poignant about this quiet, aging man. Despite all his success and his power, he seemed shy and vulnerable, almost depressed, and eager to make human contact. I must admit, I reacted. After all, this was Walt Disney, genius and entrepreneur, globally recognized, the creator of Mickey Mouse, the founder of Disneyland and Disneyworld.

At his request, I wrote down my office address and telephone number. He promised to send me a Mouseketeer kit.

He never did. Instead, late one afternoon a month or so later, without warning, our lobby receptionist rang me at my office at 230 Park Avenue, and said:

"There's someone here to see you."

"Who?" I asked.

"A Mr. Disney. Oh," she gulped. "Walt Disney."

Hurriedly, I ran down to editor-in-chief Bob Stein and asked if I could receive my visitor in his larger office instead of my smaller, messier quarters. Bob agreed. Today my old boss recalls he couldn't understand the whole situation. After getting autographs for his two sons, he packed his briefcase and went home, leaving Walt Disney and me alone.

I am not hinting that there was anything in the ensuing three-and-a-half-hour conversation that would remove its G-rating. It could have been that Disney had no other place to go—he told me he had been signing contracts all morning, and that since I seemed so interested in what he was doing, he thought I might like to hear about it. My instinct as a woman

145

told me there was more to it than that. Perhaps I reminded him of Mary Poppins: perhaps I offered both safety and enlivenment to a remote, repressed man. But some secret spring was there abubbling, however pasteurized, and I did not have the heart or the inclination to turn it off.

It was mostly a long, rambling I'll-tell-you-my-dreams monologue. He revealed that his interest in fairs and parks went back to his father, who had been a carpenter on the construction of Chicago's Columbian Exposition in 1893. He recalled his boyhood days on a Missouri farm, which sounded straight out of one of his movies.

And then Disney explained his long-range plans for EPCOT (Experimental Prototype Community of Tomorrow) which he felt would express his ideas on how the world should be run: an ordered, controlled environment with its own police force, even its own manufactured weather.

The afternoon stretched on, and only ended when Bob's secretary came in to inform us the building was closing. Walter Elias Disney kissed me chastely on the cheek and went off alone.

I never heard from him again, and he died less than two years later.

Disney's dreams about EPCOT, with some modifications, came true this October in Orlando, Florida. I hope to visit it soon and balance its reality against the plans I heard on that strange afternoon, in which the weather was controlled, but discernibly warm.

Of course, my most exciting trips to Hollywood were those associated with my seven years of doing Star Dazzle Awards on the *Merv Griffin Show*.

Merv has been on the air for twenty years. I first met him back in 1967, when he was operating out of the theater in New York, with Jeeves-like Arthur Treacher as his sidekick. Bob Shanks was the producer then, and he invited me to observe the six-hundredth show from planning to taping. I did a piece about it in my column, hailing Merv's "nimble wit and near naughty humor."

In 1975, I received a phone call from an old friend, Arnold Jurdem, one of the most forceful public relations men in town. He had several big clients, including Celanese and Simplicity Patterns, and he wanted to discuss a proposition with me. Would I be interested in doing still another awards program for the *Merv Griffin Show,* now operating out of Hollywood for Metromedia? His angle: the clients would do tie-in fashion shows.

I thought it over. I made sure we could have control of the selected stars, and that the concept would not be confused with our sacrosanct Women of the Year Awards—also that the tone of the event would not in any way demean the image of *Ladies' Home Journal,* even though I knew Merv had a firm hold on many of the women we were reaching.

Everything checked out just fine. So my second career, that of girl ham, was launched. The criteria were simple. Star Dazzle Awards were for top female stars with super-marquee value who could also find time to fit into their crowded schedules a definite appointment to pick up the award at a requested date and time on the stage of Merv's theater near Hollywood and Vine. There were no juries or reader polls. With the approval of Merv's able producers, first Betty Bitterman and then Peter Barsocchini, my staff and I would pick whom we thought were the hot ones and proceed to hound them for a confirmed acceptance. It was all great promotion for the *Journal,* naturally, and for me. But it also gave us the chance to get some first-rate cover tries backstage, where we'd have one of our best photographers ready to shoot.

And thus, for seven years, I got to share the stage with Merv Griffin for ninety minutes a year. At the beginning, I was a fish out of water, scared stiff from the second I walked out on the stage. Gradually, I learned not to fidget, to keep my eyelids up when I talked, to avoid looking at the monitor, and to relax and enjoy myself. Anyone who questions the power of Merv Griffin should find out the reaction after you've done the show. Strangers stop you in the street, stores are willing to cash your checks, long-lost relatives appear from everywhere.

Merv always made it easy for me. He can be playful, probing, and sometimes outrageous, but I never had anything but the most courteous treatment. His whole setup is organized to make guests look good: sets, lighting and camera work, and makeup artists backstage who are trained to take years and pounds off your face. Merv never meets his guests beforehand. You are interviewed beforehand by a staff member, who in turn briefs Merv. After makeup and last-minute dress changes in the backstage dressing room, you wait for your appearance cue in the Green Room, where there are reinforcing refreshments for those requiring them. You know it's all being taped, so that if you drop dead, faint, or otherwise embarrass yourself, it can be edited out. And there's a pause between segments, so that you can even run out to the bathroom if you have to.

My only real hassle came in the booking of the guests. With the help of my assistant Barbara Fortson and senior editor Jan Goodwin, each year we ran into Merv Griffin Name-Hunting Season. The quarry was easy to find, but difficult to snare. Yes, Jackie Smith and Kate Jackson and Farrah Fawcett Majors (still tri-yclept at the time) would love to pick up their awards. But they were shooting *Charlie's Angels* in northern California and couldn't make the show in time. We used some pressure on the producer and got him to finish earlier.

Gladys Knight changed her mind three times and finally, without the Pips, flew in from Vegas. Sissy Spacek arrived with a bad case of impetigo she had caught from her horse. Loni Anderson arrived garbed as Jayne Mansfield one year, and returned the next year in her own clothes to discuss her broken marriage. Bo Derek came as if costumed to play Polly Cinders. Linda Carter, Wonderwoman, sang. Debbie Reynolds did a little dance. Sally Field talked seriously about her career, until sly Merv opened the subject of Burt. We had already selected Sylvester Stallone as our first male Star Dazzle winner, but he bowed out because there was a writer's strike. Young Ricky Schroeder was declared the awardee by a technical knockout in the last round.

I had a new gown for every show, sometimes by Simplicity, sometimes by a top designer. Michael Thomas, who did the fashion shows, one year thought I deserved even more *luxe*. He sent me to Van Cleef & Arpels, on Rodeo Drive, to borrow any little baubles I cared to wear on the show. That was fun. "No, I'm not the emerald type. Have you something in plain diamonds?" My plain diamond necklace and earrings ($150,000 retail) was what I wore on the show, and hastily returned to a guard before I could be mugged on the way home.

Talk shows on TV are less sure-fire, although radio seems to be having more and more chat in its hat. Dinah Shore and John Davidson are gone, Mike Douglas is in limbo, Cavett's regular stint has been canceled, and even Merv and Johnny Carson are fighting to maintain their preeminence. I think that talking heads and recycled celebrities do have a saturation point. But these shows are lifelines for the lonely, educational models for the lost art of conversation, and a useful place to observe the passing pageant of the world's wisdom and witlessness.

Of course, electromagnetic Phil Donahue is doing fine with his mixture of titillation and audience involvement. Incest, transvestism, abortion, open marriage . . . if it's kinky, Donahue will have it, although he also delves perceptively into serious issues and books as well. Number 2 to Donahue these days is reformed blimp Richard Simmons, missionary of diet and exercise, whose boundless energy and humorous exhortations to "thin down those Hadassah thighs" has won him a devoted following. But even these formulae will undoubtedly fade in time.

Among TV's many casualties was Rona Barrett, sometimes called the poor woman's Barbara Walters, although it's a comparison unfair to both women. Rona, too, fell a victim to the system, and after much feuding and fussing had to depart both ABC and NBC and now edits an expensive gossip newsletter. At the time I met her last, she was still at the top of the Hollywood gossip heap, married to the man from whom she has since separated, and making lots of money in her sideline, real estate. I wanted her to write a piece for the *Journal* on the new business-oriented gossip, which she eventually did.

We arranged to meet in the Polo Lounge of the Beverly Hills Hotel for a late lunch. The place was jammed with the usual celebrities, and the maître d' took me to "Rona's usual table." In a few minutes Rona came in, that familiar blond head atop the tiny slim figure that reflects years of self-discipline and determination—because she certainly didn't look that way originally. She walked briskly across the room, nodding to various Names as she went. Then she slid in beside me on the banquette. Before I began my editorial discussion I said:

"It's so nice to meet you after all these years. Because I've always wanted to clear up a question in my mind. Did you ever live at 235 East Twenty-second Street in New York?"

She looked at me peculiarly.

"I did, for a short period. Why?"

"Do you remember a woman who also lived in the apartment house—a young woman who first spent months in a wheelchair and then wore a leg brace?"

Her gaze was even more disbelieving.

"That was a long time ago," she said.

"I know it was. Because the young woman was me."

And I told the story of how I had broken my leg, and been confined to the wheelchair for almost a year, until I graduated to a heavy brace. And how, finally, when the bones mended and the brace was dispensed with, I had decided to go uptown all by myself, and had hesitantly gone out to Twenty-third Street to catch a cab. And there was this girl, also waiting for a cab, whom I had noticed before.

And how we had talked, and finally rode uptown together.

"My God," said Rona. "I think I do remember." There was a long pause.

"I was heavier then," she said. Fat was the word, but I did not venture it.

"Yes."

"And I had my own problems at the time."

"Yes."

The girl I remembered had a debilitating, almost deforming muscular disease that made it difficult for her to walk. That is why we had noticed each other. In our taxi ride, Rona had told me how she was running Eddie Fisher's fan club and a TV fashion service, and I told her how I was working out of home for *McCall's*. I remember being impressed, and inspired, by her activity in spite of her limitations. For years, I did wonder if that awkward, struggling girl was really Rona Barrett. I think I mostly made the connection through the voice.

Then, as well as now, it was an emotional moment. Finally, I said, "If anyone could have told us then that someday those two handicapped people would be doing a replay here in the Polo Lounge, living the lives we both do, would we have believed it?"

"I would," said Rona decisively. "I always knew that if I stuck to it and worked hard, I'd get what I wanted."

That's Rona. Somebody told me just this week that she was

recently a guest at Kirk and Anne Douglas' home. Anybody who remembers the opening of Rona's raunchy book, *Miss Rona*, will gasp. As I say, that's Rona. She doesn't give an inch.

Crossed paths, persistent dreams, unswerving hubris, and people to whom drama comes naturally. Even in Hollywood, where make-believe is everything, sometimes truth writes the best scenes of all.

EIGHT

Washington Diary

Nobody expects women's magazines to impersonate *Newsweek* or the *Partisan Review*. But it could be that a lot of us have avoided significance by shying away from heavier subjects involving government and world affairs. At the very least, some editors say wistfully, we should be creating a climate that whets women's awareness. With females voting today at the same rate as men, it is at least equally important to educate them politically, as well as helping them to decide how to trim their thighs, what to have for dinner, whether or not to have an affair, and at what point a child is ready for toilet-training. All important topics, provided there's not an economic crisis or atomic destruction in the wings.

But reality is reality, and mass women's books must cater to their audiences and reach for sales. Once more, the emphasis is on personalities rather than issues when it comes to the Washington scene. This is not all bad. Very often, revelations of character and intimate human details provide a grasp of the big picture.

There is a recurring rhythm to the gossip themes of contemporary Washington. Nancy Reagan extravagance stories are reminiscent of old Jackie Kennedy snipes. Diana McLellan briefly supplanted Maxine Cheshire, but the Shallow Throats still are spilling the same kind of secrets. Sexual congress is still in session on the Hill, with updated permutations. Some things *do* change. George Shultz will never be as much fun to write about as Haig or Kissinger, and so far there's no duplicate of Martha Mitchell. However, the beat goes on. (And so do Nixon stories.)

A reputable national magazine cannot fool around with *National Enquirer* puffed-up rumors. Our consciences, and our lawyers, see to that.

Magazine gossip has to be bonded stuff, distilled from reliable and checkable sources—highly placed friends in the current administration, vengeful but accurate informers in the displaced group. If the budget permits, it helps to have a presence in the capital. At *McCall's,* we had stalwart Christine Sadler. At the *Journal,* the redoubtable Mary Finch Hoyt was our Washington editor for a time. Mary served as press secretary to Mrs. Edmund Muskie, Mrs. George McGovern, and Mrs. Jimmy Carter, the latter during both the campaign and the White House stint. These ladies now comprise a kind of literary handicraft circle. Rosalynn Carter's book will follow her husband's, Jane Muskie is writing a novel with Abigail McCarthy, and Mary Hoyt is halfway through her novel. Question: Will the plot lines cross?

I always felt it helped the magazine if the editor also occasionally showed up on the scene. "It's the East Wing today," I'd say with studied casualness, whipping out my driver's license at the security gate to prove I was a White House regular, blasé about it all. Which I never was. Curiosity and gregariousness led me to friendships with some of the top media women: Helen Thomas, Fran Lewine, Isabelle Shelton, Wauhilla La Hay, Kandy Stroud, Trude Feldman, and others. I also found that a working national editor had to have, at the very least, a meaningful relationship every morning with two newspapers: *The New York Times* and the *Washington Post*.

Obviously, there was a priority interest in First Ladies. Mamie, Jackie, Lady Bird, Pat, Betty, Rosalynn, Nancy: America's list of best-dressed women, all trained at some invisible academy called Our Lady of Grace Under Pressure. They should have expected what they were getting into when they married their husbands, but they could not have predicted the relentless assault of the media. I often wondered how Eleanor Roosevelt's legend would have fared under today's no-holds-barred rules that seem even worse now that she's dead and can't defend herself. Ridicule she was able to cope with; emotional exposure I think would have destroyed her.

And the First Daughters, involuntary elements of the White House image, Margaret, Caroline, Lynda, Luci, Tricia, Julie, Susan, Maureen, Patty. Indulged, restricted, sulky, sunshiny, independent, robotic, repressed, liberated, pretty, plain, talented, or a mixture of these qualities, they were American girls whose fathers happened to be successful politicians. Daughters had the better deal. They weren't married to the job, and they knew they'd get out while there was still time to recover. Some I got to know better than others, but all were candidates for our coverage.

We did not just go after the female cast of Pennsylvania Avenue. I also hummed "Hail to the Chief" as I went to press conferences, had Oval Office visits, and sat in on presidential group interviews in the Cabinet Room, where I always tried to filch a memo pad. I had a private tour of the offices with a starry-eyed newcomer named Jeb Stuart Magruder. And once, while pursuing a story involving Henry Kissinger's two secretaries whom he took to China with him—and for whom we had dresses made from the fabric they bought—I had a long, serious conversation with him in his office about his own career and the world in general.

Fortunately, I rated a few invitations to state dinners. Among them, Nixon's bash for Brezhnev, with Soviet flags eerily flying around the White House and Brezhnev himself checking out the brief-skirted girls in Johnny Mann's singing troupe. I discussed this later in the evening as I wallflowered during the dancing with a good-looking conversational partner named Alexander Haig. And then there was the fabulous state dinner the Fords gave for the Australian prime minister in a tent on the South Lawn. Betty Ford, at the height of her drug and alcohol problems, had difficulty staying awake.

Thanks to Nixon speechwriter Ray Price, whom I knew from *Herald Tribune* days, I had a privileged pre-Watergate peek at Richard Nixon's hideaway office in the Old Executive Office Building, where I saw the electronic equipment on which he played classical music . . . and taped. I never did see the tiny cubicle Johnson used as his office for eye-to-eye confrontations. It was next to the Oval Office, and Lynda later told me her father seldom invited her there, either.

My Washington saga really began a long time ago, in connection with that slogan I had created for *McCall's:* TOGETHERNESS.

In William Manchester's narrative history of the United States, *The Glory and the Dream,* he writes: "The Easter 1954 issue of *McCall's* introduced 'togetherness,' a concept which quickly became so popular that it took on the overtones of a social crusade and became almost a national purpose of the 1950s."

To propel the crusade, my boss, George H. Allen, and I plotted a series of Togetherness Award Luncheons in Washington, cosponsored by the Federation of Business and Professional Women. We gave citations to top women in the nation's

156

capital, some achievers in their own right, like Margaret Chase Smith, but mostly wives of powerful men.

One of the award winners was Lady Bird Johnson, then wife of a promising senator from Texas who was just recovering from his first major heart attack. I sat at his table, listening as he earthily described every detail of the attack, the ride to the hospital, and the recovery. "President Eisenhower had a major heart attack," I said. "You could run for President."

"My heart attack was bigger," bragged Lyndon Johnson. "And I have no intentions of ever being President."

Lady Bird joined us for a while, and I was so impressed with their obvious interactive togetherness that I wrote a short story for *McCall's* called "Winter Train," which also incorporated the blizzard I ran into on the way home. The story was about a strong senator who becomes ill, and the wife who steadfastly and subtly rebuilds his confidence. I sent it to her without comment, and she wrote me a charming letter, never acknowledging the parallel, but obviously recognizing it. I saved many other pieces of Johnson correspondence through the years, but this one I lost in the shuffle.

It was at a Togetherness Luncheon that I also had the first of many meetings with Thelma Catherine Patricia Ryan Nixon, then wife of the Vice-President. I had bought a new outfit for the event, a simple silk tweed dress from Bergdorf Goodman's, which I carried down on the train in its own box and put on just before lunch.

"That's a lovely dress," said Mrs. Nixon, as I went through the receiving line. "It's just the sort of dress I'd like to take on our trip to Ghana." President Eisenhower kept the Nixons on the road in those days.

"I bought it at Bergdorf's in New York," I said. "I'm sure you can order one."

"It's such a nice fabric, so cool," she said, touching the

157

sleeve. "Too bad, I won't have time to get one. We're leaving the day after tomorrow." I moved down the line.

In about fifteen minutes, I found myself talking to someone standing on the reception line, and got moved through again. Once more, Mrs. Nixon admired the dress, and I decided it would be a nice Togetherness gesture if I gave it to her. Explaining that it was practically unworn, I made my offer. There was some negotiation about size—she wore an 8 or a 10, and this was a 10. (I was slimmer then; she did not seem as frail.) She finally smiled and said, "That would be just wonderful. It's just what I need. If you'll take it down and leave it with our chauffeur at the side entrance, I'll be forever grateful."

Just plain straight girly-girly trading. I went upstairs, changed into an alternate outfit, and left the box with the Vice-President's chauffeur.

Newspapers and news magazines the following week printed photographs of Mrs. Nixon in Africa, but she was never in my contribution. A month later, the dress arrived by parcel post at my home. It was badly wrapped and very creased. In the box was a crisp note from a secretary thanking me for my generosity but explaining that the dress did not fit. End of story. I never wore the thing again, mostly because I could not admit to anyone that the incident had ended so gracelessly for both Mrs. Nixon and myself.

Years later, I think I finally got the point. I was doing an "interview" with the famous Nixon dog, Checkers, then living in the Fifth Avenue apartment to which the family had repaired after Richard Nixon's stunning defeat in the California gubernatorial race. Like a pro, the senior citizen black-and-white cocker spaniel posed for the photographer and me, with only a housekeeper to supervise.

Suddenly, it occurred to me that this was the clue. Five years before the dress incident, Nixon had made that classic tear-jerking speech on TV, in answer to charges that he had taken illegal contributions from a millionaires' campaign fund. He had spoken of Pat's "respectable Republican cloth coat," and the gift he had received after his nomination for Vice-President, "a little black-and-white spotted dog our little girl Tricia, the six-year-old, had named Checkers . . . Regardless of what they say, we're going to keep it." He had turned a bombshell into a triumph with a cosmetic apologia.

All of which led me to an Art Buchwald-type fantasy re-creation of the scene that might have happened the night of that Togetherness Luncheon.

"See what a nice lady from a magazine gave me," says Pat to her husband. "I'm going to take it to Ghana."

Richard Nixon looks up from his desk.

"*What?* You took a gift from the press? No way. Remember that last flap."

"That was your problem," says Pat. "I want to keep this dress. It's pretty. And respectable."

"No you're not," says Dick, handing it to a secretary. "Send it back to the magazine woman with the thrift shop complex. Make it perfectly clear that we are not accepting it. Say it doesn't fit."

That situation nicely clarified in my imagination, I left Checkers chewing one of his master's slippers, which I had found under a bed. I probably should have put it back where I found it. But I let the dog keep it. (Later, of course, I deepened and revised my opinion of Pat Nixon.)

One of the other Togetherness winners was Perle Mesta, the former minister to Luxembourg and Washington hostess whose idea of Togetherness was a two-party party. Some years later, she agreed to be a regular columnist on *McCall's*, if I would shape and write her columns. Thus Perle Mesta became the hostess with the ghostess, and I started to visit Washington on a routine basis.

Perle was a dynamo, people-shrewd and warmhearted. She was also one of the earliest supporters of the Equal Rights Amendment. Many of the parties I helped her to plan and run made the news as well as the good columns. Jane Russell joined us at a WAIF party in the Washington zoo; Senate Majority Leader Mike Mansfield was given a dinner in his honor. There was a belated birthday party for Lady Bird Johnson, and I scouted down the gift at an autograph shop: a valuable O. Henry inscription in his own handwriting: "The more wrinkles a woman acquires, the smoother she becomes." Lady Bird still treasures it.

The biggest whoop-de-doo was the week in which LBJ, celebrating his fifty-sixth birthday, was nominated for a full term in the presidency. He had hesitated about making the run: Scathing criticism had hurt him and he was afraid he could not unite the country. He had already written out a statement rejecting the nomination and had asked Lady Bird to review it. In one of the most historic and beautiful love letters of our time, she wrote to Lyndon Johnson:

Beloved:

You are as brave a man as Harry Truman—or FDR— or Lincoln. You can go on to find some peace, some achievement amidst all the pain. You have been strong, patient, determined beyond any words of mine to express. I honor you for it. So does most of the country.

To step out now would be *wrong* for your country, and I can see nothing but a wasteland for the future. Your friends would be frozen in embarrassed silence and your enemies jeering.

I am not afraid of *Time* or losing money or defeat.

In the final analysis I can't carry any of the burdens you talked of—so I know it's only *your* choice. But I know you are as brave as any of the thirty-five.

Washington Diary

I love you always.

BIRD

He listened to Lady Bird (who had been roughed up in the previous issue of *Time* magazine) and decided to accept the nomination.

And so Atlantic City in August 1964 became in Johnson's words "a place of happy surging crowds and thundering cheers." Perle took over a huge wedding cake villa in Ventnor, New Jersey, ten miles from Atlantic City's Convention Hall, from which she transported guests to nightly parties in buses marked "Perle Mesta's Party Line." As usual, I worked for the entire week behind the scenes . . . and my picture ran in *Time* magazine.

There were 200 guests a night, press, politicos, celebrity volunteers. Muriel Humphrey, wife of the man Johnson was to select as his Vice-President, was co-hostess on one of the evenings. This was also the week in which I met Lynda and Luci, as well as Jack Valenti, today head of the Motion Picture Association. Then he was the man who set the standard for staff loyalty by proclaiming, "I sleep each night a little better, a little more confidently, because Lyndon Johnson is my President." (Valenti also married LBJ's former secretary, Mary Margaret.)

I attended Convention Hall proceedings, where there was a strong undertow of Kennedy rue and sadness under the Johnson bandwagon rah-rah. The assassination wound was still aching. The keynote speech was delivered by Senator Pastore of Rhode Island.

A friend and former *McCall's* associate, Stanley Frankel, along with his brother-in-law Newton Minow and others, pulled off an amusing coup at the Atlantic City convention. Goldwater had put up a huge sign on the million-dollar pier near Convention Hall to provoke the Democrats. It read "In

your heart you know he is right. Vote for Barry Goldwater."
Stan and his cohorts managed to put up a small sign just
below it: "Yes . . . extreme right." It was the talk of the
boardwalk until Goldwater forces had it removed.

Wednesday night, Perle ran a huge dinner dance at the
Hotel Claridge, with entertainment arranged by composer
Dick Adler. Eddie Fisher sang on a dead mike, but the rest of
the ball was noisy and star-studded. In the lobby, I ran into
two convention celebrities: Martin Luther King and his wife
Coretta. They had been our Riverdale neighbors the previous
summer, and after we compared political notes, they asked for
everyone back in the community, particularly some of the
youngsters who had been their children's playmates. It was
warm and pleasant; no ominous premonitions.

Many seeds were planted that week. But mostly it was the
beginning of a deeper relationship with the Johnson family,
especially Lynda, whose gratifying personal growth I have
watched with affection over the past eighteen years.

Lynda Bird Johnson Robb, today the wife of the Governor
of Virginia, activist in her own right, mother of three daughters, handsome, gracious, poised. It's difficult to remember
the awkward teenager in loafers and bobby socks whom I first
saw in 1964, then met again when she came to work at
McCall's in 1966 when Bob Stein, the editor, decided that a
President's daughter on the staff would make some extra
waves for the magazine.

"We're going to treat you like any ordinary editor," Bob
told her. But the publicity was enormous, the press conference
drew throngs, and Lynda was always under heavy security,
protected by Secret Service men.

My office was at the other end of the building, but Lynda
used our slight acquaintanceship to find it. This was chiefly
because I was the one who could show her *Women's Wear*,
Variety, and the other show-biz and gossip publications that

162

were currently chronicling her romance with George Hamilton. George, who had already starred in a few movies, was also using his darkly handsome charm and quasi-social connections to be seen in the right places with the right people. He had been the guest of the Henry Fords' daughter, Charlotte, at their Southampton, Long Island, house, and when Lynda came to stay at Charlotte's New York apartment, she met the man who became her escort throughout 1966, causing great ripples in the press and many uncertainties in her family.

It is difficult to find out how disturbed they really were about this romance which seemed to change Lynda's life by giving her a whole new confidence in herself as a woman grown. Luci, the younger daughter, was bubbly, outgoing, irrepressible, with a deep religious streak which eventually brought her to Catholicism. Lynda was the product of a strangely neglected childhood. Lady Bird couldn't be a bad mother if she tried, but her busy life was centered on the politicking of her husband, and Lynda as a child was largely brought up by her grandmother.

As she moved into her late teens, Lynda had a number of beaux. But not until George Hamilton did the real lights switch on. Whatever his motives, his attention and affection and theatrical knowledgeability made a difference. He took Lynda to George Masters, the Hollywood makeup man, and had her hair and face restyled. Her clothes improved, so that *Women's Wear* stopped its cruel jeering. Her sense of fun emerged.

Lady Bird's book, *A White House Diary*, first mentions George on January 1, 1966. On January 23, Lynda is studying for her finals at the University of Texas, and Mrs. Johnson writes,

Lynda thinks she is doing pretty well . . . She interrupts a telephone call from me to say, "Mama, you'll just have to wait, George is calling." He is part of the wine of life, exciting and heady.

On February 20, Lynda is in New Orleans, with George, chaperoned by Lindy Boggs. Her mother notes:

Purposely, I kept from calling Lynda . . . I didn't want to interrupt Lynda's independence or her time, or seem like a hovering or concerned mother. I balance between try-ing to remember that next month she will be twenty-two, with the right to independence, and that her father is President of the United States, and that anything she does will reflect on him.

Nobody knows how the romance was finally closed out. George went to Lynda's graduation, and was seen with her at the White House and the Johnson Ranch well into 1967. Then, on August 10, 1967, in the White House, Lynda crept into her parents' bedroom and said, "Mother, Daddy, I am in love. I want to get married." The man was Chuck Robb, a Marine captain with six years of service, currently serving as a military aide in the White House. Again, in her mother's words: "They like doing the same things. And this from Lynda, whose interests have been turning more and more these last two years to people on the stage and screen, café society people, people who are very rich, or very talented or very social. Chuck Robb, on the other hand, looks like the 'All-American Boy.' Wholesome, handsome, masculine." Fourteen years later, Charles S. Robb won as the Democratic candidate for Governor of Virginia, and Lynda became the second presidential daughter to be First Lady of that state. (The first was the oldest daughter of Thomas Jefferson.)

Mrs. Johnson's last annotation about George in her diary—

outside of brief mention of him as a guest at Lynda's wedding—is a note less than a week after Lynda's declaration, when she went into Lynda's White House bedroom.

I noticed something different, and for several moments I couldn't decide what it was. And then I knew—gone, gone, gone were all the pictures of George Hamilton— the romantic-devilish one on the chest of drawers, the patrician-handsome one, and lots of other little mementos—a faded telegram pasted on the mirror. She hadn't said a word about it. They had simply been removed.

I have always felt Lady Bird Johnson to be one of the most admirable First Ladies we have ever had. "I would not like to be exactly like her," wrote Lynda. "She is too disciplined . . . She has a strong sense of duty that I inherited only in part." As the wife of LBJ, Lady Bird faced more personal and public pressure than any of the others except, perhaps, Pat Nixon. But she never lost her composure or tact, never crumbled, never forgot the basic courtesies. If she paid an inner price, if she suffered pain, remorse, or resentment, only she knows, and probably will never tell. Even as the critical biographies proliferate.

Lynda stayed on at *McCall's* while Chuck went to Vietnam. There was one bad morning when her Secret Service men received a rumor that he had been killed in battle (he was always a prime target). But by the time the rumor reached her, it had been proved to be just that.

Lynda and I both phased out of *McCall's* at about the same time. When I became established at *Ladies' Home Journal*, we became friendly again, and this is when I really began to see the potential in this remarkable young woman. She became a *Journal* contributing editor, but this time, she said, "I really want to work, and learn to write. I want assignments that would stand on their own under any by-line."

165

She was no longer the incumbent President's daughter, but she was still a celebrity. It fell to me as editor, chaperone, and hovering substitute mother to go along on some of the assignments, mostly to protect her in sticky situations. And we had some great adventures.

In 1972, Lynda became an American Airlines stewardess for a day. (She had considered being a flight attendant when she was graduated from the University of Texas, but it was obviously impossible.) Lynda spent three tough days at the Flight Services College in Dallas, living with the other candidates. Then she flew Flight 76 from Los Angeles to Washington, as a stewardess, her only "disguise" a wig, worn because her own long hair did not conform to regulations. She served in first class; I flew tourist. It was a routine flight, and one of her "co-stews" gave her full marks. It also made a great story.

An even better story was "I Remember J. Edgar Hoover," by Lynda Johnson Robb. She had known him since early childhood, when he lived across the street from the red brick house on Thirtieth Street in Washington where the Johnson family made its home when LBJ was first a congressman and then a senator from Texas. J. Edgar Hoover rarely granted interviews, but Lynda said, "If we talk about nothing else, we can talk about dogs. He once put our lost beagle on the FBI's 'Most Wanted List,' and he also once gave us a dog named Edgar."

I went with Lynda on the interview, which was scheduled for the morning of May 2, 1972. (An earlier date had been suggested, but Lynda couldn't get a baby-sitter for her two daughters.) We walked through the FBI building to the office of the Director, where we were met by an aide, H.P. Leinbaugh. The appointment was for ten in the morning, so we sat down, had coffee, and started to wait. Mr. Leinbaugh kept leaving us to make telephone calls, and we watched the clock moving further and further past ten. Finally, at 10:30, Mr.

Leinbaugh came into the room and said to Lynda, "I am sure you are accustomed to keeping secrets."

"I certainly am," said Lynda. "And so is Mrs. Hershey."

Mr. Leinbaugh looked around uneasily.

"I must swear you to secrecy. I am sorry to say that Mr. Hoover has passed away. He died in his sleep this morning and we are not going to release the news for another hour."

"May I call my father?" asked Lynda. "He's at the ranch."

"Perhaps you'd better use the coin phone outside," suggested Mr. Leinbaugh. Which she did. But LBJ had already heard the news through his Secret Service agents.

We stayed until after noon, requested a photo of the two little cairn terriers with whom J. Edgar Hoover had shared his breakfast every morning, and left in an atmosphere that was very different from the one we had walked into a few hours earlier. Lynda wrote a fascinating article, which was featured on the cover. (Yes, she did her own writing, with very little editing required.)

Lynda worked on the *Journal* for almost ten years, again leaving when I did, chiefly because she had started to work for her husband's gubernatorial campaign. Her daughters are growing fast: Lucinda is fourteen, Katherine twelve, and the baby, Jennifer, an active four. Although she was far from enthusiastic about hitting the campaign trail when her husband ran for governor, she gave it her all. And today as I watch her with her children, and with her husband, and with all her own activities, I still have this sneaking suspicion that someday, somewhere, she is going to hit the campaign trail for herself. After all, she's not even forty, and that mixture of her mother's and her father's abilities is not going to be wasted.

I have been to the Johnson ranch in Texas on several occasions, but I remember one most acutely because of Lynda's sister, Luci Johnson Nugent. After LBJ left the presidency, I discovered that Luci was anxious to write the story of Yuki, the small white mongrel dog that had become her father's "best friend" during his last year and a half in the White House.

The abandoned Yuki was picked up by Luci near a Johnson City gas station and adopted. He was named Yukimas, the Japanese word for snow or white, but the shortened form stuck. After a troubled puppyhood, he began to develop talents, including the ability to "sing," which Lyndon B. Johnson cultivated into a dog-human duet. Eventually Yuki left the Nugents, moved into the White House, and followed LBJ into retirement.

"Not since my mother died has anyone or anything been as devoted to me as this dog," Luci once heard her father say. "He even is a substitute for my wife when she runs all over the country now." He said this with a pointed look at Lady Bird, who listened with a smile.

Through Luci and Yuki, I became involved in the production of the story, and spent a day or two at the ranch with all three major characters. I had the grand tour with LBJ in the white Lincoln Continental, I up front with him, Luci in the back, and Yuki draped on the back of the seat between us. (The dog took to me; that helped.) Johnson showed me the Johnson birthplace, the animals, the cemetery where he would someday be buried. Once he stopped the car to pick up a piece of Kleenex some tourist had dropped on the road. Mostly, I remember him nodding and lip-moving along with the taped commentary as he walked me through the birthplace—and the satisfaction with which he showed me a copy of the August 1908 *Ladies' Home Journal* in the magazine rack. It was a glorious ride, matched only by another I took a few years later alone with Lady Bird, who drove me through the back acres of the ranch, with a beautiful commentary on the history of the land, its flora and fauna, and how much it had meant to her husband and herself.

Washington Diary

I kept up with the Johnsons through the years. My husband and I attended the opening of the Library, and I also was involved in the dedication of the Johnson memorial in Washington, D.C. Lynda in recent years has made several TV appearances with me and for me, and as her interest in the women's movement became strong, we appeared on various platforms together. A friend of mine, Varina Steuert, and I gave Lynda and Chuck a fund-raising party for his campaign, and someday soon I'm going down to see her in the governor's mansion. Luci, of course, is now divorced from her husband and lives with her four children, Nicole, Rebecca, Sara Claudia, and Lyndon, the oldest. She had a frightening bout of serious illness last fall, but I think she's snapped back with her usual bounce.

Interestingly enough, I became almost as friendly with the Nixons when they moved to the White House.

It really started in June 1969, when I was invited to join a three-day First Lady trip with Mrs. Nixon and her twenty-year-old daughter, Julie Nixon Eisenhower, to visit volunteer projects on the West Coast. Tricia stayed home to get ready for her visit to Britain and the investiture of Prince Charles.

It was Mrs. Nixon's first solo excursion, and my first big White House junket. Every reporter paid a pro-rated fee. The plane was filled with tough, wisecracking reporters, who called Pat Nixon "a Barbie doll" behind her back, and who were suspicious of the political implications of the volunteerism pitch.

We were constantly harassed by antiwar demonstrators. Once, I got caught in a shower of strips of paper reading "If this was napalm, you would be dead." But nevertheless it was exciting, stimulating, and a revelation. Because the spirit imprisoned in Pat Nixon seemed to stir and flutter before our eyes as she reached out in genuine contact. The human situations were heart-stirring: a literacy center, a community garden center in an inner city pocket, a day care center for migratory workers, a volunteer Braille operation at a Jewish temple. But it was at the Foundation for the Junior Blind in Los Angeles that even the most cynical reporters melted. The kids, all sightless, presented scenes from *The Sound of Music*, and then embraced Pat. She did not hang back. Somehow this exposure broke through all the plastic barriers of her persona. She hugged, she touched, she wept. Pat Nixon convinced us all that she had a capacity for caring. She was finding herself in her own feelings, and it was gratifying to watch. By now, the remote lady who had returned my dress was a long-forgotten apparition, and I came home with a sense of admiration for what Pat Nixon was, and what she could ultimately become: her own woman. If the man she was married to didn't trip her up. Which he did.

For the February 1972 issue of the *Journal*, we decided to ask Mrs. Nixon if she would cooperate with us on a fashion feature. She said she would, and we began to work on an exclusive story, using moderate-priced clothes from American designers, including an opulent Chinese-print evening gown by Donald Brooks. (We offered her the dress to take to China, but her staff director refused, this time graciously.) Pat Nixon proved to be a cooperative model. Despite a heavy cold and a cough, she came to photographer Otto Stupakoff's midtown studio for two days of sittings, and gave us happy, poised fashion pictures that were a hit with readers.

Once more, I decided to do the interview myself for the personality profile which accompanied them. I called it "The 'New' Pat Nixon," and it is based on about four hours of conversation I had with her in the yellow sitting room of the White House private quarters. Reread today, it is a doubly sad piece, for it is obvious that it was one of her best times. "No matter what you think of her husband," I quote a Democratic woman at that time, "you've got to be happy for what looks like the emancipation of Pat Nixon. She worked all her married life to help him get where he wanted to be. Now she's enjoying her own job."

And she was. The protective layers still made her one of the best question-parriers in the world. (This was before Nancy Reagan took up the title.) But she did answer many of my questions with spontaneity, confirming for me that she had met Richard Nixon when they were both acting in *The Dark Tower* in the Whittier Theater Group. I also got a glimpse of spunk and independence, a child whose mother had died when she was thirteen. She had worked her way through a variety of jobs: secretary, X-ray technician, department store executive, teacher, and movie extra.

Before I did the interview, one of my nervier press friends said, "Get her to talk about the menopausal nervous breakdown she had when Dick lost the election in California in 1962. She is supposed to have recuperated at the Annenbergs', which is his big debt to them."

I never did. In my article, however, I did include a paragraph saying: "There are those who said something had happened to Pat Nixon, that even her steely spirit was crushed at the time in a woman's life when she is perhaps most emotionally vulnerable." I do know that even though I called him "relentlessly ambitious," Richard Nixon wrote a letter commending the *Journal* on the profile and saying it was one of the best ever done on her. I did not make his "enemies list."

Somewhere about this time, a Catholic magazine did a profile on me, and asked for my secret ambition. I have always loved Ireland, and from the very first visit, felt a strong spiritual pull to the beauty of the land and the contradictorily joyous and tragic moods of its people. "I would like to be the first Jewish woman ambassador to Ireland from the United States," I told the reporter. When my answer was printed, the wires picked it up and the Washington papers carried it. Her press secretary, Helen Smith, called me and said Mrs. Nixon had shown her the clipping and told her to inquire if I was serious. I was, but not for realization at that time, in that administration. But I was impressed that she noticed.

It was during the Nixon administration that one of the most dramatic incidents of my magazine career took place. It was before I became editor-in-chief—John Carter was still in the job—and I'm willing to share with him the "almost miracle" we didn't quite pull off: the negotiation for POWs at the height of the Vietnam war.

It was part of our "Power of a Woman" campaign, this time aimed at a problem deeply troubling the nation: the 1,500 Americans who were missing in action or prisoners of war in Southeast Asia, constant focus of both the antiwar groups and the establishment. In the *Journal*'s Christmas issue, we ran a small petition for readers to sign as citizens, asking the Vietnam forces—all three factions—for identification, neutral inspection, and repatriation of the sick and wounded. *Journal* readers responded in a flood of replies: 65,000 of them in all. It was off the normal course of a women's magazine, but we suddenly realized that we had an instrument for peace in our hands. I went down to the State Department and talked at length to Frank S. Sieverts, who was handling POW problems. Would it be at all helpful if the *Journal*, even-handed, nonpolitical, sent a delegation to the Paris peace conference and showed these letters to the Vietnam representatives?

The State Department was more than mildly interested, although everything had to be nonofficial. In April, the *Journal* ran an open letter to the leaders of Hanoi, the Vietcong, and the Lao Patriotic Front. We told them we would like to present to them what the women of America felt about the need for peace, and we asked that a committee of women, selected by the *Journal* on an impartial basis, be allowed to visit the prisoner-of-war camps.

172

In April 1971, our delegation went to Paris—one of the most interesting missions of my lifetime. There were four of us, John Carter, myself, Myrlie Evers, the compelling, compassionate widow of Medgar Evers, the slain civil rights leader, and Virginia R. Allan, dignified and diplomatic, the former president of the National Federation of Business and Professional Women's Clubs. (She later went on to be an active member of the State Department herself.)

It was April in Paris, and we made our headquarters at the Hotel Raphael, near the Arc de Triomphe, right across the street from where the peace talks were being held. With us were several copies of a big bound presentation: "The Women of America Speak Out on Prisoners of War and Peace in Southeast Asia." Bernard Valery, staff correspondent of the *New York Daily News* in Paris, cheered us on.

"I know it's far-fetched," he said. "But you people just might make a breakthrough on this whole POW question. Everybody in town knows you're here, and they could very well latch on to your delegation as a neutral mechanism for getting some movement started."

As we sought for personal meetings with each of the three delegations, their obstinacy was overwhelming. I logged 68 phone calls, not to mention letters and telegrams. We went to the official headquarters of Hanoi and the Lao forces and camped outside their doors. I pleaded in my fractured French and we had an interpreter to make sure our message was not misunderstood. Finally, on Thursday, Myrlie Evers rose to her feet on the floor of the peace conference's daily press briefing and gave an impassioned speech is resonant contralto tones. Nguyen Thanh Le, Hanoi's press representative, answered her with a twenty-five-minute prepared statement, but then came down to the floor to talk to us all in what one bureau chief called "the most human communication of the peace conference."

173

Myrlie Evers went alone to see the top assistant of Madame Binh, head of the Vietcong. Myrlie left our presentation book, along with twelve gold charms inscribed with the *Journal*'s theme, "Never Underestimate the Power of a Woman." The presentation was abruptly returned the next morning; the charms were kept. I sometimes ponder about who's wearing them now.

The real problem was that this was the week President Nixon decided to resume the bombings in Vietnam, increasing the rigidity and hard-line attitude of the Viet representatives. Looking back, I marvel at our temerity in even attempting such an ambitious project. It didn't work. But as we said to our readers in the magazine, "Let the record show that at least we tried."

The years spun on. The Vietnam war finally drew to a close. Watergate took center stage, and the Nixons left, followed by the Fords. I have always liked Gerald Ford, and once rode on the presidential press plane down to Jacksonville, Florida, for his historic meeting there with President Anwar Sadat of Egypt. The setting: Epping Forest, home of Raymond K. Mason, head of the Charter Company, for which I still work. Later, as Betty Ford faced and met her problems, I visited the Fords at their Vail home, and had some frank discussions with her on how the election had been lost to Jimmy Carter.

The Carters. I met them at the first Democratic convention in New York City: Lynda interviewed Rosalynn for the *Journal*, arranged by Mary Hoyt. I also had breakfast with Amy and Miss Lillian and guessed that both of them were going to be unsettling new experiences for the American public. I worked with Rosalynn on ERA; and with President Carter on a number of projects. I always felt his interest in putting women in top positions was sincere and effective. As for the rest of it, I admired his intelligence, but suspected that his uptight, down-country style and his awkward body-language would undermine his achievements.

In the November 1980 elections, just before I moved on to new duties, another opportunity for special service surfaced.

The League of Women Voters was having difficulty arranging its traditional TV debates between Carter and Reagan. Working with my capable friend, radio's Sherrye Henry, we rushed into the vacuum with a new idea: a "Presidential Candidates' Dialogue With Women," cosponsored by the *Journal* and the Women's Economic Roundtable, with 100 other women's organizations involved. We ran a full-page ad in *The New York Times* urging both major candidates to bring their case to American women. But it didn't work. They had their one debate, under League sponsorship . . . and the election determined the winner. Once more, we tried.

As women gain more and more clout on their own in the Washington arena, the old question arises: Will we ever have a woman President, with or without a First Husband in the background?

Maybe not tomorrow. But somewhere out there, there's a political science major who needs no assertiveness training. She was president of her class and ran the student council. After she goes to graduate school, she plans to run for the state legislature, then on up through lieutenant governor to governor. She's learning the ropes of her local political machine, and of her party on the national level. She's making lists of fat cats and important media people. She looks great on TV but is studying her videotapes to see how she can improve. She's tough, energetic, and though she likes men, does not have marriage in her immediate future. She has, she says, other plans.

Look around. There are many like her already on their way. Never underestimate their power.

One of them *could* make it.

NINE

Blind Items and Double Exposures

"Were there ever any cocaine busts at *Ladies' Home Journal?*" a young man asked me at a party.

Tongue secure in cheek, I replied: "I think you're confusing us with *Good Housekeeping*. I hear they cut the stuff at the Institute."

Such flipness would flop at Hearst Magazines, where the most compulsive addiction is making piles of money, and where to trifle with the *Good Housekeeping* seal is to raid the ark and stomp on the golden calf.

Even more shocked would be any remnants of the old days at Curtis Publishing, home of the *Saturday Evening Post* and *Ladies' Home Journal*. Back then, I am told, the mood was always correct, haughty, and vigilantly WASP. No unharmonious outsiders could lay a hand on the family periodical jewels.

Today's magazine offices are still more Peg Bracken than brackish, but they are increasingly democratic and casual. Residual snobbery has faded; smarts, not social standing, get and keep the job. There is a new kind of clannishness, however. The Women's Media Group, "the new girl network," which meets regularly at the Four Seasons, is, according to one member, "a ferocious clique: power sets the rank." In magazine offices themselves, the ambiance is more relaxed. The group socializes, swaps movie preview passes, exchanges rumors, and passes around photocopies of the *Media Industry Newsletter,* a trade tipsheet which seems to have a wiretap in every top magazine office in town.

Though semicozy havens, women's magazines are not all sweetness and light. There is also a goodly share of mavericks, free spirits, rebels, offbeats, eccentrics, and sometimes even lawbreakers.

There was, for example, that famous ad director at *McCall's* who had to go to jail for nonpayment of his income taxes. The elderly *Journal* editorial assistant who was the soul of respectability until someone discovered she'd been quietly embezzling thousands of dollars for years. Before the IRS cracked down on business expenses, there were more accepted forms of upper-level plundering. Top editors and publishers thought nothing of charging all sorts of goodies to the company. Patios were added, even entire new homes built, on the magazine's budget—with a photograph or two in the magazine to justify the expenditure as an editorial contribution. Props from photography sittings were considered part of the *lagniappe.* Sometimes a whole moving van would stand at the ready to transport furnishings and accessories directly from the studio to the editor's or the art director's home.

Today, there's still some scrambling for beauty product samples and leftover fashion accessories. But the loot is nothing like it used to be. Manufacturers, caught in an economic squeeze, loan or rent their merchandise on consignment and demand it back before greedy fingers can reach out. Companies that seduced editors at Christmastime with baubles from Tiffany or Cartier now send contribution cards for the heart or cancer funds, amount unspecified. Or they proffer gift-wrapped packages of their own products.

Junkets and far-flung freeloading have been cut, too. There is a Pillsbury bake-off every other year, but food editors no longer get to Hawaii for "The Pineapple Classic." Editors who supervise travel columns still pick up a free trip now and then. But the movie industry doesn't lay on what it did in the sixties and the seventies. I recall a three-day premiere party in Paris, hosted by Walter Reade, that was wall-to-wall glamour, all for some clinker about a little boy and wolves. Walter is gone, and so are the wingdings. There are still press screenings, and some parties for charity, but that's it.

Creative people being what they are, there is some free-floating temperament at women's magazines, and the weather forecast of intermittent emotional thunderstorms is always a safe one. Ordinary people suddenly become focuses of violence and notoriety. A *Redbook* cover girl becomes involved in a front-page murder case. A fashion model from the same magazine, the girl who did the Blue Nun commercials, dies with her lover in a New York apartment. A motherly production editor is discovered to be the author of pornographic novels in her spare time. A prominent editor of a home magazine has a fight with her live-in companion, locks him out of their shared quarters, and the brouhaha hits the tabloids when he sues to regain his possessions. Much, much later, they get married. Today she uses his name on a new and important job.

Even the private lives of conservative employees are abruptly ripped open by circumstance: accidents and serious illness, painful breakups and divorces, children snared in the tragically familiar traps of drugs and delinquency. Once, I estimated that 80 percent of my staff were in or contemplating psychiatric therapy. I wondered how the other 20 percent were hacking it.

And then there's that inevitable debbil, sex in the office. The old Adam and the new Eve scamper about the bosky dells of both business and editorial. The best stories are vintage ones, however—executive secretaries "kept" by affluent bosses, innocent girls with beguiling bosoms seduced by loutish junior executives. Bosses and bosoms persist, but there are fewer innocent girls and new laws against sexual harassment. Pursuit today is reciprocal, and unless pillow-talk favoritism really disturbs the pecking order, workplace relationships are shrugged off as part of the territory.

I have even encouraged a few couplings myself. My most notable matchmaking: the introduction of Amy Levin, then the *Journal*'s articles editor, to Art Cooper, editor of *Family Weekly*. He was divorced, she was the widow of another great editor, *Redbook*'s Bob Levin. Art and Amy clicked, and I clucked like a mother hen at their wedding.

By blending in some of the older chronicles with the new, a pungent mix is produced. To protect my friends, and myself, however, I'll go the Truman Capote route and treat them as blind items.

Let us consider first that fading breed, male editors of women's magazines. They wouldn't have been where they were if they didn't have a sensitivity to women's interests, but they also were strong, ambitious personalities. To them fell an unspoken *droit de seigneur* over their staffs of able, intelligent, and largely adoring women. Since most of them were already hard-core husbands and fathers by the time they arrived in the candy store, their reactions varied with their susceptibilities, which in turn varied with the amount of sugar content in what they went home to at night.

Some took temptation in stride and kept a circumspect distance from all libidinous fringe benefits. Some just flirted. ("Male editors tend to be great kissers; that's it," attests a female editor who once wrote a novel on the subject.) Some became bullies and tyrants. One in memory had a continuous harem of handsome, brainy, and politically conscious hand-maidens who seemed only too eager to serve their guru in all ways.

No man is an island, and even if he is, there's always a ferry. A small percentage of the editors did get emotionally involved with a young woman who hit the right nerve endings and stirred up the right hormones. (Fiction and fashion editors seemed to have the knack.) Since most of the men were married, liaisons were deviously plotted like intelligence maneuvers. Meetings were often set up in other cities, or other countries. Secretaries were provided with cover stories and trained to avoid specific details on locations.

Few of these idylls lasted. In the end, home and children and job security triumphed over passion. The men stayed in place; the women mostly moved on.

There was no predicting who would be caught up in an extramarital affair. Sometimes it was the most sober stick-in-the-mud who fell the hardest, seeking his last fling before the onslaught of paunch and prostate problems, looking for something more in life than monthly deadlines, commuter trains, and orthodontia bills.

"You could always tell when a man was having an affair," said one of the wise contributing editors. "He'd start using a hair stylist instead of a neighborhood barber. He'd break out into Gucci shoes and belts, and change his restaurants to ones with subdued lighting. His teeth and gums would supposedly collapse, necessitating two-hour dental appointments several times a week, from which he'd never return to the office. His mood swings would be radical, from agony to ecstasy. And we'd all have to do his work. It was a relief when things blew over."

If they did.

Alcohol as a social lubricant in the magazine business is too

181

often a given, with some people getting more lubricated than others. Back in the Otis Wiese days at *McCall's,* there was a special luncheon table set aside for editors in the old Park Lane Hotel. Here Beefeater martinis would be consumed with incredible rapidity, turning afternoon meetings into soggy debacles. When Norton Simon, the West Coast financier and art collector, bought *McCall's,* he put in Arthur B. Langlie, a former governor of the state of Washington, as head of the company. Editor-publisher Otis Wiese resigned, taking eighteen other staffers who followed him like lemmings into the sea, and it was high tide at the Park Lane, with just a few olives floating in the gin. To add insult to injury, Governor Langlie turned out to be a teetotaler.

Every magazine has its store of drinking stories, with most of the bacchanals concentrated on sales meetings. Veterans of one book recall intemperate orgies which ended in showers of flying glass and the summoning of the police. (This was also the women's magazine whose owner had a private bathroom wallpapered in erotic patterns. When a communications conglomerate took over, the paper was changed.)

At the *Journal,* I never protested about the imbibing, although I always wondered why executives had to give rambling speeches when thoroughly tanked.

I was more teed off on another subject. *Golf.*

If anyone were to ask me how a magazine could get into a hole, I would suggest it might be hit there by a four-iron. Golf's a nice game, fun, relaxing, and I recognize that a lot of important business can be conducted with customers on a fairway.

But enough is enough. Outside of the news magazines and the sports field, the *Journal* was the most golf-obsessed publication around. "The Open Checkbook Open" I call the ceaseless round of golf outings which, at a minimum cost of $30,000 each, were supposed to attract revenue to our pages. In addition, various executives were allowed to put their country clubs on their expense accounts.

As a budget-squeezed, space-hungry editor crying for dollars to invest in my product, I felt putt-upon. For ten years, Arnold Palmer has been listed on the *Journal* masthead as a Contributing Editor, earning more than many of our senior working editors. He was there ostensibly to impress advertisers, among whom a chosen few were selected to play with him at Bay Hill and Latrobe. Maybe golf outings do work. Striding up to the awards table in patchwork print pants and red blazer to be honored for a low gross or low net, being able to brag that you played with Arnold Palmer, may have some influence over your choice of the *Journal* as against other magazines. But I always was convinced that the many dollars (and man-hours) siphoned off into golf could have been used more effectively in editorial or at least in sound selling strategies.

Joe Ostrow, executive VP of Young and Rubicam and a media force in the ad world, says, "This kind of old-fashioned ad-selling made a lot of people buy a lot of dumb things because of the conviviality. Today's buyers are more involved in the scientific aspects of marketing."

Once, I put through an editorial project which I thought might bring the charismatic Arnold Palmer closer to our readers. We created a letter contest for women golfers, and eight were picked to join "Arnie's Army" at his Bay Hill Club in Florida. The article, when we ran it, was tested in our normal focus-group sessions. It scored as one of the least-noted, least-read features in our history.

Proving that I am self-serving, I was less exercised about the *Journal*'s sales department's participation in tennis. I am a tennis buff, so that our sponsorship over a number of years of a portion of the Forest Hills matches did not displease me. Here, I had an opportunity to watch, and meet, a young Chris

Evert, Rod Laver, Arthur Ashe, and many of the other top players of the time.

Fortunately, the new owner of the *Journal*, Bob Riordan, is a runner. That form of exercise can be done, inexpensively, in a park or on a marathon course.

My editorial life has coincided with the administrations of seven Presidents of the United States. At the *Journal*, I also lived through—and survived—the stewardship of seven presidents.

One was named Tremble. I use his real name because he made few things quiver, and departed quickly, leaving me the fine desk at which I still work.

Another company president was supposed to be a tough guy, who reputedly did make some of his minions tremble.

For years, I am told, there was a graffiti above the urinal in a Second Avenue restaurant called Goodale's, before it moved further downtown:

"If you get them by the balls, their hearts and minds will follow." The wit and wisdom of ——— ———.

Since I always found this particular president a crew-cut pussycat, I never understood what they were talking about.

Another company president was a chronic Mr. Malaprop, whose misapplied words and phrases didn't prevent him moving to the top—often. Introducing an editor who had worked on the introduction of Revlon's Etherea perfume, he declared, "She invented Urethra!"

Another time, he found fault with the "bon mutts" I used as cover lines. At important dinners, he asked his public relations adviser to make sure he was on the "deeus." Dais, deeus, he still has a lot of industry fans, and may good luck be with him on his new big job after a few unlucky years.

Still another company president and I had some clashes

over the course, but we could always dissolve our differences on the dance floor. He was a natural-born hoofer, and he never stepped on my toes when the music started to play. Proving that underneath it all, we were still good partners. And continuing good friends today.

There are many more tales about publishers, ad directors, and ad salesmen, their strengths and their weaknesses. But they all gave so much to the *Journal* that, as a special dispensation for the magazine's one-hundredth birthday, I have crossed any extraneous past history out of my notebook. Except for one item, which is truly a blind item, since I do not know the identity of the person concerned.

He was one of the magazine's self-declared studs, the kind who looked at girls as if he was undressing them, and bragged to the other guys about his prowess as a lover.

I am sure that my most prurient curiosity was not particularly served by this knowledge, but a reliable source informed me that his medical records contained the notation: "Undeveloped genitals." (Please don't call. Records have been shredded, and for further diagnosis, you will have to rely on personal examination.)

Am I going to be sexist and leave the women unscathed? Of course not.

First, the good news.

Just a decade ago, women chief editors were a rarity. Today, the list is considerably longer. There are many of us, on small magazines and large, all over the country. But here is my list of the all-star eleven, women whose own effective personalities and viewpoints have been stamped on their successful publications.

Myrna Blyth: Shrewd, dynamic editor of *Ladies' Home Journal*

Helen Gurley Brown: She *is* the *Cosmopolitan* girl

185

Elizabeth Crow: Thoughtful updater of *Parents Magazine*

Mildred Istona: Chatelaine of Canada's crisp *Chatelaine* magazine

Amy Levin: Incisive, impudent sparkler at *Mademoiselle*

Kate Rand Lloyd: She put *Working Woman* on its solid course

Grace Mirabella: She has moved *Vogue* from pure fashion to a wider world of insight and contemporary appraisal

Paige Rense: The sophisticated force behind *Architectural Digest* and now *Bon Appétit* and *Geo*

Geraldine Rhoads: The original tower of strength at *Woman's Day,* now editorial director

Patricia Ryan: The female person behind *People*'s sustained excitement

Ruth Whitney: The heavyweight mind that took *Glamour* out of the lightweight division

Although they are more entrepreneurs than editors, a list of female icons must also include Pat Carbine and Gloria Steinem of *Ms.;* Cathleen Black, publisher of *New York* magazine, Christie Hefner, the new doyenne of *Playboy,* who has to reconcile her feminism with bunnyism, and Judy Daniels, who carved the executive women's magazine, *Savvy,* out of a personal dream, and is now at Time, Inc., working on some new dreams.

Do these top editors have common traits and personality patterns that might hint to others the path to success? Here are some of the ways I see them as being alike:

Vitality: Their nonstop energy is one of the biggest things they've got going for them. These are gung-ho go-getters whose enthusiasm ignites quickly and seldom fizzles out. They can make rapid-fire decisions without flinching. Challenge stirs up their adrenaline: An opportunity, a new author, a hot property unleashes freshets of vigor. To conserve stamina, they prioritize, dealing with some crises immediately, allowing others to cool off. They learn how to hang in for the long-distance run. But they have to stay in front all the way, because by now winning is in their blood.

Creativity: Their riverbed of ideas is never dry. Brain cells are always making new associations, pulling fresh inspiration from everything—a clipping, a song, an overheard comment, something on the business pages. They are word-coiners and concept-innovators. But they must also be disciplined, organized planners. The sheer weight of their duties demands that they compartmentalize, coordinate, schedule—always with an eye on the total product, which they think of as their own.

Editorial Skills: Above all, they know their craft . . . every part of it. They understand typography, production, circulation techniques. They have a fervent but appropriately disinvolved interest in the success of the advertising department. They cultivate a good graphic eye, but can direct an art director without crowding him or her. As hands-on editors, their blue pencils can cut away fat and bring a central point to the fore, or add the zing that turns a dull cover line into a teasing puller. If pressed, many probably could step into the shoes of any of their editors, and some secretly believe they could write all the articles as well.

Firmness: Top editors vary in physical appearance and manner, but all of their spines are reinforced with steel. They didn't get where they are by being powder puffs. That baby-doll voice may belong to a jungle fighter: Watch out for the rabbit punch from that little manicured hand. But the best ones are also sensitively people-minded. Occasional impatience and imperiousness are canceled out by the knowledge that inspiration and leadership get more out of a staff than tyranny.

Awareness: Top editors have richly furnished minds. They are students of society, watching for the changes that affect their readers, bathing in the mainstream but also dipping their toes in the underground springs. They are avid readers, for pleasure as well as business, go to the theater, the movies, concerts and the opera, museums and galleries, the ballet. They watch TV, both network and cable, to keep in touch—and some even admit they enjoy it. Social circles are important, too. A wide circle of contacts and friends, of different ages and interests, keeps the pot boiling. Many a great magazine idea is born at the dinner table.

Personal Identification: Women's magazine editors know their readers' lives because they've been there. Many are married, some have children, which helps on the women's service books. Those who edit to working women also have lived through struggles in the professional and corporate areas. All have private relationships which often impinge, and are not always smooth and easy. But they cope, and conciliate, and face facts, and adjust, and grow, just the way they tell their readers to solve their relationship dilemmas. And somehow, they make it, using their own advice.

Image: Most recognize the need to increase their own visibility, for their magazine's sake as well as their own. Self-promotion in some cases can get to be excessive, but most women are learning to cope sensibly with public speaking, TV appearances, and advertising presentations. The smart ones get help in perfecting communications skills and in finding the right personal and fashion image. This is not narcissism. It is also perceived as good business.

Resiliency: Top women editors are not invulnerable. Their

hearts sink with bad newsstand figures, their spirits slump at management difficulties beyond their control. But as veterans, they bounce back. There's always the next issue to reverse a trend; the magazine business usually turns out to be self-renewing. If it were all just a breeze, it wouldn't be as much fun. And if you can't stand the heat in the kitchen, you shouldn't be a chef.

And now for a bit of mild bitchery about women editors in general, up and down the masthead. True, these classifications could just as well apply to men, but since most of the staff is female, we put them in that gender. Incidentally, I see myself in quite a few of these composite types.

The Angster: Anxiety and guilt are her lines. She goes into a decline on the wrong side of a closed door: Her doom is undoubtedly being sealed within that room. She worries constantly. The story isn't going to pan out, the art department is missing the point, the photographer is messing things up, the plane will be late or crash, her sniffle is about to develop into pneumonia. She broods that she is getting nowhere in her job; perhaps she should change and find something else. Praise and comfort don't help: Her masochism won't allow her satisfaction. She's hard to take, but if angst and compulsiveness are her MO, and they work, endure. Angsters often make it to the top.

The Maneuverer: Also spelled *man*euverer. She's the slick operator who always sidles up to the top man at an office cocktail party. She has confidence in her abilities, but she prefers to hurry things up with political strategies, seductiveness, and if necessary, horizontal war games. If this Machiavellian manipulator works for you, get her number early and let her know you're on to her game. ("In this company, we don't go right to the president. We work through channels.") Or be less subtle. ("He usually calls up a few weeks later and asks me to fire anybody who gets too close to him.") Sometimes maneuverers pull their devious ploys from without. One well-known editor approached me for a top job with friendliness and flattery. I asked her to do an analytical memo on the *Journal,* which she did. But she also did another one—highly critical—and sent it to the head of the company. P.S. She didn't get the job, obviously. Ambition is admirable, provided it has some minimum standards of sportswomanlike behavior.

The Breeder Reactor: She is the office gossip hub. Insecure, she gets a sense of power from being the first to retail today's hot rumor. She will usually come into your office and, in a conspiratorial whisper, lay on a blockbuster revelation about someone in the company, or some shocking corporate plan in the works. Most times, she is a mile off base. But once in a while, her info is on target. How does she do it? One of her talents is reading memos upside down on peoples' desks while carrying on a normal dialogue. She can eavesdrop at fifty paces on conversations and telephone calls. She is not above snatching glances at appointment calendars. And she has a network of others exactly like her on the jungle telegraph. Outside of renting her out to the CIA, there's nothing much you can achieve by trying to cut her off. Make a deal. If she hears anything really good, let her share it with you first. In return, you'll keep her informed. It may work out to your advantage.

Madame Chic: Skipping quickly over drabs and slobs, we come to the woman on the staff who specializes in elegance. Always exquisitely groomed, she is a silent reminder to all of us that we haven't had our hair frosted, that we haven't done our isometrics, that we really should go to Saks or Bendel's or Bergdorf's and get a fashion consultant to lick us into shape. Her clothes bear top designer labels: De la Renta, St. Laurent, Adolfo, Blass, Beene, Calvin Klein. Her boots are gleaming, her purses seem to come from an endless repertoire of Gucci, Fendi, Vuitton, and the other beloveds of affluent bag-ladies. As she walks down the hall wafting clouds of Ivoire or Opium, one envies her classic fashion touch, her assurance, her supplementary income. But one also wonders what the hell she is doing on this job. Why isn't she just meeting Nancy and the girls for lunch at Le Cirque?

Ms. Chic: She's the young wonder, the trendy, savvy fashion shopper who always knows where to gear up with the new looks at a price. She's the first to wear legwarmers, browbands, longer skirts, shorter skirts, antique dresses, sweater dresses, running shoes. She knows where to get Perry Ellis-type sweaters for a fraction of the price, and may even wheedle her mother into using her needles and knitting one for her. She stalks offbeat boutiques in remote sections of town, Army-Navy dealers, secondhand shops. Her jumpsuits always fit as if molded, zipper lowered to the cleavage point. She has more rings than fingers, feathery or close-cropped hair, and a desk drawer filled with makeup. She'd rather shop than eat, and she's fun to watch. She's undoubtedly a good worker, too—she has her eye on a bulky fur, and she can't swing it without a raise.

The New Corporate Woman: She may not stay in editorial long; she's out to learn the ropes and someday own the whole caboodle. She's taking management courses and has an application in for business school. Her conversation is studded with buzz-words like "parameters," "research intensive," "implementation." More than any of the other editors, she hangs around the word processors

191

and the computers. If it's not a pose, and she's serious, help her find her way into the management area of the company. You could end up working for her someday.

The Prima Donna: Every editorial office has at least one. She comes in late and leaves early. Has to have the office with a window. Is always up in arms at a real or imagined slight. Won't enter a room where people are smoking. Gets exercised about injustices in other departments; is tough on her own staff. Schedules her vacation at the most inconvenient time, and can't change her reservations in Sardinia just because there's an emergency. Stages major temper tantrums at least twice a year because of some minor rebuff in her area. Demands exorbitant raises at every review period and supposedly has a backup job if they are not met. You have to be almost indispensable to be a certified prima donna, or you wouldn't carry on that way. But every gravy train eventually runs out of meat stock. Prima donnas, if they don't deliver, can end up singing in the chorus. Or in the backup job.

There are lots of other types:

The Eager Beaver: The junior who can't wait to move up gradually, but tries to tell you how to run the magazine before she's learned to file.

The Ice Maiden: Cool, cool, cool. Nothing flaps her, nobody gets close to her. She does her work, period, and goes home. Behind the mystery may be a vacuum: on the other hand, *she* could be the one who's really making it with the top executives.

The Ardent Feminist: She's still in there fighting, making sure that sexism doesn't rear its head. Babies must be she as well as he. There should be more on abortion rights in our pages. The cover puts down women. Important to have around, as a kind of group conscience, even if occasionally irritating.

Earth Mother: The shoulder you lean on for a good cathartic cry, dispenser of psychic chicken soup, organizer of baby showers and retirement parties. (Her desk drawer also has the needle and thread, and first aid supplies.) Every organization should hire one, if she's not already on board.

One category has been omitted because it strikes so close to home: The Talker. I admit, I am a happy chatterer, a teller of stories, a verbal sharer of excitement. Although I am practiced at confidentiality, I have undoubtedly broken a few embargoes and let a kitten or two out of the bag, to the consternation of Howard Greene, who usually guided my press relations. However, there is one journalistic adventure (the "double exposure" part of this chapter title) which demonstrates that I can both control my tongue and shoot from the lip. It is the saga of *Ladies' Home Journal* and Patty Hearst, and to my knowledge nobody has ever recounted it before.

Between the time of Patricia Campbell Hearst's kidnapping by the Symbionese Liberation Army in February 1974, and her arrest by the FBI on September 18, 1975, she was the subject of the most massive womanhunt in the nation's history. Because of her involvement as "Tania," photographed holding a carbine in a bank robbery, she was considered a criminal as well as a victim. There were no answers as to whether she was brainwashed or a willing convert. Although her parents Catherine and Randy Hearst (since divorced; he has remarried) stood by her, the rest of the public was more skeptical. Her elusiveness proved embarrassing to the FBI: twenty-two months was a long period in which to stay lost with a whole country's best sleuths looking for you.

One afternoon in July in the summer of 1975, I received a telephone call from literary agent Sterling Lord.

In hushed tones, he told me he wanted to discuss a momentous journalistic coup: the possibility of an exclusive personal interview with Patty Hearst somewhere in hiding. I gulped disbelievingly, and arranged for an early meeting in my office with Sterling. Because of the heavy legal overtones, I decided it would be safer to have a partner in all the negotiations. Thus, executive editor Dick Kaplan and I together were thrust into a period of high excitement, half suspense movie and half comic opera, which is still difficult to sort out because of the elements involved.

Sterling Lord was representing Les Payne, a black reporter on *Newsday*, a Long Island newspaper, who had done some writing on the SLA, and who came with good credentials. He was reputed to have some good contacts in the SLA: they probably were William and Emily Harris, or "Teko" and "Yolanda," as they were called in the movement. There was also a photographer on the team. And a mysterious third party lurking in the wings, who was somehow a key to the puzzle. Much later, I found out who he was.

Jay J. Armes, from El Paso, Texas, is an unbelievably colorful character who was once billed in *People* magazine as "the nation's top private eye." With that name, pronounced "arms," he is armless, using two hooklike appliances that can do anything, including firing a .22 magnum shell from a revolver built into his right prosthesis. Armes, who claims he has never lost a case and charges million-dollar fees, once found Marlon Brando's kidnapped son in four days, and, more recently, recovered a thirteen-year-old Canadian boy, kidnapped to Greece, by sending in his own twelve-year-old son to escort the boy out of school.

Armes, he told me recently, was willing to provide the location of Patty Hearst (he also claims to have SLA contacts) for the trifling sum of half a million dollars. Less than half of this was going to be put up by the *Journal*. The rest would be filled out by book, syndicate, and foreign rights. Japan had already bought in.

There was just one problem. The FBI had spent more than eight and a half million dollars looking for Patty, and to have information about her whereabouts and not turn her in made one subject to criminal proceedings.

Before we got down to discussing the details, I rode down one morning from Riverdale to Manhattan in a taxi with a woman friend, ad executive Janet Wolff, and discussed my dilemma. Was it worth risking the magazine's reputation for this sizzling scoop? Somewhere along the line, I mentioned the name Patty Hearst. I forgot that taxi drivers have large ears.

Within an hour, the FBI was in my office, asking me to spill everything I knew and impressing upon me my responsibility as a lawful citizen.

"Look, Mr. Johnson," I said, hoping I sounded like a character in a TV series, "I can give up this story now and you can follow it around town, or we can make a deal. This is a great American magazine, in a patriotic company, and we are not about to do anything unlawful. Wouldn't it be better if I moved this along as I would any other story and then you can do your normal thing?"

He said he would let me know. He called me back in two hours, agreeing. By the end of the day, I am positive that Dick's and my office phones, as well as our home phones, were tapped. Callers complained of oceanic sounds and

195

sputterings, and I would always explain that there was something wrong with the equipment.

With the approval of our management and our lawyer, we specified that we would pay only on receipt of a bona fide interview, with answers to our own submitted questions, to be confirmed by photographs, handwriting, and voice-print.

From then on it was cloak-and-dagger all the way. The FBI as an unseen presence was a given. Sterling Lord was put under surveillance from a window across the street from his office, and he was also photographed by a "tourist" as he walked across Central Park. If we all met, it was on a street corner where there was a noisy excavation going on. Dick's friend in the police department told us that long halls were bug-proof, so our staff tried to figure out why Dick and I kept walking up and down having hush-hush conversations. The project was assigned a code name: the Barbara Howar manuscript. Barbara Howar, a friend, was another client of Sterling's. But she never knew we used her name.

Best of all, I liked our elaborate system of phone communication. We wrote down the telephone numbers of a long row of pay booths in the back of the Waldorf-Astoria Hotel. When Sterling called us, from another pay booth, we were to go to the Waldorf and wait for one of those phones to ring. Madness, madness. It was either Robert Ludlum or Woody Allen—I'm not sure which.

What happened? Was it a scoop or a scam?

Again, a reconstruct. Jay Armes today says that his lawyer told him to balk because Sterling Lord was asking for 30,000 words. Les Payne claims now that "there was more than just a chance that the interview would take place, but a lot of complex things went wrong." We had everything in readiness: a check in escrow, a special printing arrangement, a voice print from a radio broadcast against which to do a comparison. (Fortunately, no real bucks were ever spent.)

And then Patty Hearst was apprehended. Jay Armes recently told me that the real breakdown of the project came because he wanted a federal agent present at the interview, a condition which the rest of the team would not meet. He also says that he then gave his information away "for free."

"You mean you tipped off the FBI?" I asked him on the phone.

"I said I gave it away for free," he responded, laconically.

When I heard the news of Patty's capture, I was both relieved and disappointed. Dick and I had this lingering fantasy of somehow turning her over to the authorities right there in the *Journal* offices. Now it was all over.

But life goes on, and a good editor is always on the track of another story. Sterling Lord also agented the works of lawyer F. Lee Bailey, who was chosen to represent Patty Hearst at her trial. He offered us a book, *Patty Hearst: The Untold Story* by Bailey and John Greenya, and said it would be delivered soon after the verdict. Which it was. But since F. Lee Bailey lost the case, and since Patty went to jail, and since none of Bailey's material was earthshaking, the book wasn't very good. In fact, it only ran in two parts in the *Journal* and was never published in book form.

Now comes the sequel.

In the fall of 1981, I was subpoenaed by George C. Martinez, a lawyer representing Patty Hearst. Despite her grant of executive clemency by President Carter after two years in prison, Patty Hearst, now living with her husband and daughter in California, was bringing an action for a retrial. Her request was based on the fact that F. Lee Bailey was writing a book during the conduct of the trial, and therefore was involved in a conflict of interest.

My testimony was taken on December 11, 1981, in a conference room near my office. Mr. Martinez had a court stenographer transcribing every pearly word. There was also someone present from the Department of Justice. One thing about my nonexistent relationship with Patty Hearst: It sure set me up in some theatrical situations.

Larry Levine, Charter's able lawyer, briefed me ahead of time. He urged me to give short, concise answers and above all not to volunteer anything.

My memory was almost blank about the book; most of the details had been lost in the flow of events. I found a record that showed we paid $40,000, which wasn't much for a major property, and I did have the actual edited manuscript, which proved how skillfully Dick Kaplan had cut it to make it more readable.

But the tenor of the Hearst lawyer's questions irritated me as an editor and a writer. Trying to insinuate that F. Lee Bailey would hang back because he was writing a book, with someone obviously helping him on the book's preparation, was nonsense. I waited for my chance to sneak in my disapproval, and I finally spotted an opening.

"Why was this book never published?" asked Mr. Martinez, in tones suggesting it was a conspiracy.

"Because," I said primly, "he lost the case. If he had won he would have had a best seller."

I was under oath, and I truly believed it to be so. I'm surely Bailey knew it, too, and thus had an added incentive to give everything he had to winning the case.

Some months later, *The New York Times* ran a news item to the effect that Patty Hearst had dropped the action and was not going to pursue the F. Lee Bailey tack.

"I'm sure your little stab had something to do with it,"

said Larry Levine. "It was the gut of the whole claim. Remind me not to call you as an opposition witness."

I concede that sometimes I speak too impulsively, am too quick with a quip. Words can hurt, damage, and knock plans awry. But sometimes the side of the angels gets just what it needs: a *talker*.

TEN

Hershey's Helpers

Plunge into the self-help mix of any women's magazine and change your life. Learn how to diet, keep trim and taut, find a job, a man, a houseplant that needs no sun. How to save your money and your marriage, how to recognize the symptoms of every disease in the medical books. How to improve your skills in needlepoint, nutrition, and negotiating. How to be more successful in the bedroom and the boardroom.

As glib writers boil down even the most complex concepts into fast-food reading, women pile their plates high with hints and tips.

Sex a drag? Try the All-New-Hit-the-Spot Arousal Plan, with diagrams. Self-confidence sagging? Be assured that "*You Are Better Than Anybody!*" Bothered by cosmic mysteries? Get the picture in a nutshell: "Guaranteed Guide to Life: Be Born. Live. Die." A klutz in the kitchen? Keep posted on calories and cholesterol, such fashions as green peppercorns, and nouvelle recession recipes that help you and your family live hand-to-mouth.

Counsel gushes from every page. Much of it is attributed to experts, real or self-proclaimed. Some insights cut close to the bone of contemporary problems: tensions and stress, the hard-pressed homemaker, the perplexed parent, the lonely single.

Other pep talks treat life as if it were hair, needing only a quick styling and a conditioning rinse to make it manageable.

Adult education is pervasive these days: books, TV, cable, radio, and universities are all into it. But magazines were there first and still continue to do the job with the most intimacy and variety. If a few readers are jolted by the explicitness explosion, many more find uninhibited candor illuminating and comforting. (The *Journal* horrified everyone in 1906 with its campaign against venereal disease.) True, when it comes to sex, instructed may not always mean ecstatic. But ignorance stopped being bliss a long time ago.

All of which leads me to my own random collection of helpers: how-tos and observations gleaned from years of personal and professional coping, some deeply serious, some laced with levity.

Please help yourself from the buffet.

Having It All

I like a good California Chardonnay, steak Diane, ripe French Brie, *Masterpiece Theatre*. But I also relish light beer, hamburgers, cottage cheese, and that dumb, habit-forming show, *Family Feud*.

I wouldn't mind owning a black sable coat to match a chauffeur-driven Rolls Corniche. But I'm comfortable riding around in our old green station wagon wearing my Snoopy sweatshirt.

Automatic elevators make me lonely; telephone answering machines with cutesy messages leave me cold. But I do warm to computers. I'm prepared to learn Basic, Fortran, Cobol, and Pascal and find my own soft spot in software. I am also considering the purchase of a word processor.

When I spill bacon grease, I've been known to spit out a certain epithet. But I don't like to hear women using that other four-letter word to vulgarize their own lovemaking.

Skillful erotic writing can turn me on: John Cheever, Judy Krantz, even those obligatory bed-between-the-bullets passages in detective stories. But my hormones are resistant to gratuitous nude gymnastics on the screen in crowded theaters.

Mary Cunningham and Lady Di have done well for themselves. But I would not switch places with either of them for all the Royal Crown at Mary's Seagram empire, or all the crowned royals at Buckingham Palace. (They can keep Bill and Charlie, too.)

Yes, I can be wistful and envious. There are chances I've missed, paths untaken, experiences I wish I'd had. Part of me would like to start all over again with Jessica Lange's face, Jane Fonda's muscle tone, and the personal courage of a hundred women I know who fight on undaunted, for themselves and the things in which they believe.

I have fantasies. This time around, I might walk a bit on the wild side, make movies with Spielberg, hang-glide, have a few more children, and live at least another century to see how it all works out. Since I'm compelled to take it from here, I'll do what most women do: continue to dream, but reach for the practical.

Nobody really has it all.

Not even the new breed of female powerhouses, with their multiple career-family expectations, their driving desires, their tough-minded juggernaut juggling on "the fast lane."

In my book, the most you can handle is a rich, satisfying assortment you can put together your way, at your pace, to savor while the savoring's good, and to share with people you love.

The rest is a matter of keeping the barnacles scraped off the hull. Of praying for fair winds. And of sailing forward, prepared to ride out both calm and rough weather.

A Paragraph of Prevention

If my daughter were nineteen now, I'd rather have her read an article in *Mademoiselle* that enables her to say to her partner, "I'm worried about herpes," or "What do we do for contraception?" than have her come home with a venereal disease or an unwanted pregnancy.

True, I would hope she would discuss her options with me, and I'd prefer to think her inherited values would prevent her from having to face any of these possibilities.

But we're not living in *Andy Hardy* or *Leave It to Beaver* days, and sometimes a magazine can get a message over a lot more realistically and forcefully than even a loving family. Although it's nice to have a lifetime subscription to a loving family.

Tears, Idle Tears

At work, in your personal life, it's a gritty, tough world. Some women feel that tears are helpful confrontation weapons, but I think they should be used judiciously, if at all. ("You can be moistureproof for ten years," said an office-wise friend of mine. "But the guys will always remember the ten minutes when it rained.")

When I was nineteen, I was interviewed for a job by the head of one of the nation's most important lecture bureaus. He wanted someone to escort his big-name clients to their speaking dates, and I gave him all the reasons why I was right for the job. When he told me I wasn't mature enough, the droplets started oozing from my eyes.

"Come back when you've learned not to cry in public," he said. "We need someone who at least looks unflappable."

Actually, it took me years to conquer my quick-crumpling tendencies, and to become more of a cool-hand fighter. Tricks I learned: taking deep breaths, for one. Retiring from the scene to formulate a strategy. "Let's cut this discussion short. I'd like to think about it before we both make a decision we might regret." Emergency move: "I guess I really don't understand what you're saying. Would you mind repeating it again?'' And always, an awareness that if you lose control, you're in a less favorable bargaining position.

Never let them see the salt in your eyes. Or if you're a man, the quiver in your jaw. Even if you're fired, flunked, insulted, rejected, abandoned, threatened, put down, passed over, or merely told you're the wrong sex or too old or too young . . . keep your powder dry.

If you must cry, do it alone, behind closed doors.

The Parenting Heartbreak

The majority of my friends (and readers) have seen their efforts rewarded with sturdy, stable sons and daughters who make their own way—maybe not always in the preferred traditional direction—but who at least show some return on the care and devotion invested in them.

But what about the others: the ones mothers and fathers sometimes won't even talk about? There are the boys and girls who do not seem to catch hold of life, who reject its challenge and find outlets in punk clothes and Mohawk haircuts, drugs, drink, drag-racing, destructive relationships, violence, crime.

Or the children who seemed so promising, but who end up without joy or purpose. Or the one child in an otherwise achieving family who cannot find himself or herself, who despite every outstretched hand becomes more and more disconnected. And the tragic few who handle anger and depression with the desperate act of suicide.

I have seen so many examples of all these children, and of aching, self-blaming parents. Single-family heads seem to bear more guilt than others. "If there were two of us, it would not have worked this way."

The truth is that if children turn out badly, there is not always a *mea culpa* cause. Our kids are not necessarily messed up because we worked or stayed at home, because we gave too much or too little, because we moved to the suburbs or remained in the city.

Raising children in this complex world is more intricate a responsibility than ever. And human nature is no more predictable.

The Bible and *King Lear* gave us a somber view of parenthood long before there was peer pressure or rock music, or a set of behavioral guidelines provided with every bassinet.

There always will be children who go astray for reasons beyond grasp, and parents who let their kids down because of undefinable pressures.

Fortunately for the human race, few people look at the odds in this emotional lottery. Couples go through tortuous procedures in a quest to conceive; explore fertility rites from temperature-taking to test-tube birth. Children continue to be the yearned-for hostages to fortune, the most glorious gamble on earth.

If you are lucky, offspring can bring you pride and pleasure as well as love. If fate has dealt you a difficult child, you must never give up. But you also cannot let this fact ruin your life.

Still Together

I don't care how many chins-up articles I have edited about new attitudes towards divorce. I've suffered through the split-ups of enough of my friends and readers to know that sundering a marriage is bound to be a rotten, destructive experience. And it's happening to one out of every two marriages in the United States.

Fortunately, the stigma has faded. Sometimes I feel that the tables have turned and that having a long marriage nowadays stamps you as uncourageous, unhealthily dependent, old-fashioned. "Haven't you ever considered breaking up?" my husband and I are asked as each anniversary rolls around.

Of course we have. We are quite dissimilar in our personalities, and we both have had to accommodate to changes in ourselves, and in the patterns of our life together. Fortunately, our basic values are a good match and we have trust in each other's reactions. But I am still the kind who does *not* put the toothpaste cap back on the tube, and Sol, exact and exacting, considers this a critical point . . . as it might be, if the toothpaste tube were an anesthesia machine.

Over the years, we have had both interesting and boring squabbles over this and other issues, most of which reflected other stresses and tensions in our lives. It has occasionally crossed both our minds, I am sure, that diversification might have its compensations.

But we've hung in, talked things out, fought our way through the triumphs and disappointments of the years. Now, as we see some friends' marriages broken up by death, we try to make the most of time. We look at our shared home, family, friends, memories, and interests with a new greediness, an autumn intensity. Our physical and mental companionship, well-worn as it is, has plenty of sparks left.

The Hersheys are still scrapping, so this may not be the final word. But I think we'll stick it out.

He just bought me a new wedding ring.

All I had to do was hint.

Women's Most Loathed Words

* Lump
    as in breast, gravy, blind date, pillow
* Late
    as in period, trains and planes, payments, lunch dates
* Lost
    as in man, cause, earrings, gloves, job, contact lens, identity
* Lonely
    as in morning, noon, but mostly night

Most Cherished Words

Love and lucky and "Let's."

Progressive Dining

Most of my mother's homemaking seemed to have been driven by conscientiousness. But when it came to entertaining, she was wholehearted and giving. As they said in those days, she laid a good table. When I was six, classmates used to like to come home with me for lunch because she fussed with such simple but pleasing effects as her "jewel dessert," multicolored cubes of Jell-O, topped with whipped cream. This early tribute to General Foods was no doubt the inspiration for all those gelatine molds I have experimented with through the years, in which a wild medley of fruits, vegetables, and other ingredients have been committed to aspic.

Her birthday parties were always productions. She would go to Dennison's and find the latest crepe paper nutcups, party snappers, and pin-the-tail-on-the-donkey games. Again, the spread would be the talk of University Avenue and would be crowned by her famous icebox cake. I have long since lost the recipe, but I know it came from a women's magazine.

I carried on the birthday celebration ritual and, in the modern suburban tradition, amplified it. For our daughter Jane, there was one party in which a real Indian princess came in her squaw outfit and told stories. For another, an authentic Maypole, which my husband and I worked on for weeks, and around which twenty small girls interlaced ribbons to music until the whole thing became hopelessly entangled. Another year, my friend Charmian Freund and I combined forces and budgets and gave a joint birthday party for her Debby and our Jane. We hired eight hansom cabs in Central Park and took

208

the whole class for a ride, followed by lunch. The two girls even had matching dresses.

The Hershey house in Riverdale was built by us for easy, casual entertaining, and we have had as many as 150 people at our big parties, mostly holiday buffets. We also have at least two or three cookouts in the summer on our terrace, and some smaller dinners throughout the year.

Occasionally, I will dip into some classic French or Italian recipes, but mostly I am an improvisational and nonchalant cook. I like to keep things easy and simple, but I'd rather err on the side of abundance than on insufficiency. I hate those collations where everything is white, bland, and skimpy, little hunks of chicken in cream sauce on toast points, finger sandwiches, plates of packaged cookies. Today, with the wide variety of prepared foods, catering services, fancy supermarkets, and other sources, there's no excuse for anyone to serve dull food.

I have some specialties, and one of them is right out of a can: B&M beans which I doctor with gobs of molasses, Worcestershire sauce, dry mustard, and a slug of bourbon (in the beans, not in me) before I put them in a medium oven for a half hour before I serve them.

Then there are my gelatine molds: crunchy ones with vegetables, or fruity ones with pineapple, or cranberries, or canned black cherries, or whatever else I decide on that morning. For a buffet, I'll have a large rare roast beef or a turkey precarved. One hot casserole: paella, Chicken Tetrazzini, or a salmon-and-noodles bake. Or Swedish meatballs, which my sister-in-law Fan prepares for me when she visits, and stocks in our freezer. At least one platter of German cold cuts, with assorted brown breads, for people who like extra food through the evening. In the summer, when we barbecue, Sol prefers marinated flank steaks which he slices thin, London-broil style. For dessert I've been known to make a berry pie with a

209

prepared shell. Otherwise, we pick up fresh pastries and a ricotta cheesecake from a local Italian bakery. Cheese and fruit, of course. And wine from Sol's creditable cellar.

For the last few winter parties, I've been serving that acknowledged cliché, fettucine primavera, from a Four Seasons recipe. Frankly, I edit this, too, preferring to sauté the vegetables a bit before I add them. But here's the original recipe.

Four Seasons Fettucine Primavera

1½ lbs.	Fresh pasta cut in ¼-inch strips
4–5 qts.	Chicken stock, well seasoned
2 tbsp.	Butter
¼ cup	Shallots, finely chopped
2 cups	Heavy cream
1 cup	Zucchini, sliced fine
1 cup	Carrots, sliced very fine
1 cup	Broccoli fleurettes
½ cup	Broccoli stems, sliced fine
1 cup	Red pepper, peeled and diced ½-inch
1 cup	Fresh asparagus, cut in 1-inch lengths
1 cup	Spring cabbage or kale, diced ½-inch
12	Basil leaves
	Salt and pepper
½ cup	Parmesan, grated

In a large pot bring chicken stock to a boil and add the fettucine and all vegetables. Bring to a rolling boil for 2–3 minutes.

Sauté the shallots in butter. Add the cream and reduce to half.

Drain pasta and vegetables well. Pour into the cream.

Shake pan well to coat the pasta. Season with salt and pepper. Pour into a preheated serving dish and sprinkle with Parmesan cheese. Serve at once.

*   *   *

With food a national preoccupation, and entertaining no longer judged by the golden candelabra on your table or the fact that you yourself slaved all day in the kitchen to produce a totally coordinated dinner, everybody should try to find his own style of hospitality. Maybe it's as informal as beer and pizza after the local football game, or a round-robin gourmet club in which you and your neighbors rotate evenings in different ethnic traditions. Maybe you want to use your inherited silver and glassware; but prefer to have handsome large paper napkins instead of linen ones (I often do). The point: Do it your way, but do it with a flair.

My daughter, who lives with her newspaper-editor husband in an apartment with a tiny kitchen, amazes me with her creative culinary skill. Sometimes I feel the chain of generations as I watch her using a fifty-year-old cast-iron frying pan my mother donated from her kitchen when I got married, and which, sentimentally, I passed along to Jane.

My mother used it for potato pancakes. I used it for crêpes, very big in the fifties and sixties. Now Jane uses it as a wok for sukiyaki and stir-fried vegetables. Cuisines change, but the link between food and family emotions goes on, like a progressive dinner.

When You're Being Photographed

Pictures of ourselves are important, whether for family memories, or for publicity use. As a chronic critic of my own photographs, and an editor who never yet has worked with a star who was completely satisfied with a cover shot, here are a few pointers I've picked up along the way.

* Relax. "Make friends with the camera," model agency director Eileen Ford has always told me. "Look at it, talk to it—at least, mentally. The less uptight you are about

211

facing that lens, the more relaxed your picture will come out."

* Dress the Part. Bachrach, the photographers who do portraits of all the top executives, tell men to wear dark, pin-striped suits with white or light blue shirts, and regimental-striped or small-pattern ties. Men like to be photographed in the morning, when there's no beard-shadow. Women, on the other hand, prefer the afternoon, so they can have their hair done.

For women, it's a good idea to bring along at least two outfits: both in light colors, with flattering necklines that frame the face. Makeup for color should be gentle: for black-and-white, it can be more exaggerated. Use a matte foundation, and blush to heighten cheekbones. "Mascara never hurts," says Eileen Ford.

* Ask the photographer to shoot a preliminary Polaroid. We always do this in magazine shots. Discuss lighting with him or her, too. Bachrach says that men like strong contrasty lighting. Women, however, should opt for softer focus. And don't scorn retouching, even if there's an extra cost. It's cheaper than plastic surgery.

* Candid Group Shots. If flashbulbs start to pop, be aware. When the photographer says "Talk to each other," resist if you're asked to show your most unflattering profile. If you're over thirty-five, smile. It helps with those stern creases around your mouth. As my public relations maven, Charlotte Kelly Veal, says: "Try to work yourself into the center of the picture. That way, the photographer gets you at a straight angle, and you won't get cropped by a photo editor. Turn slightly sideways, with your face forward. You'll look slimmer."

Word Mines

Besides a good unabridged dictionary, there are two

desk-side books I recommend to would-be writers and editors.

One is *Roget's Thesaurus,* the famous book of synonyms and antonyms. If sifted through often, it is a bottomless treasure chest of gems ready to be set with your own lapidary skills.

The other is a complete volume of Ralph Waldo Emerson's essays. Whenever I need a surprising quote or a fresh tack in thinking, I just pick a page by this old sage and find the right depth charge to stir up my mental processes.

Raymond K. Mason, head of the Charter Company, for which I work, is an even greater Emerson fan than I am. RKM reads something from RWE almost every day.

When You Go Public

Because of their jobs, community activities, or political involvements, more women are climbing onto the podium these days to give informal or structured speeches.

I have come a long way since the night I had to introduce a panel at a Neighborhood House Forum and was convinced that I would faint midway through my two-minute task. But many experiences in public speaking have given me know-how and confidence. Here are some of the things I've learned.

* Jump In and Say Yes. If the speaking invitation sounds like something that can be useful to you, your cause or your job, say you'll do it. Remember to check for conflicts on your calendar, and get specific details on what you'll be expected to do. Start preparing early, with research if necessary. If there have been other recent addresses or papers on your topic, write to the person who delivered them for a copy of his remarks—or notes. Most speakers are delighted to answer this type of request.

* Case the Situation. Make sure you have all the facts on location, audience, other speakers, and time you will be required to fill. Will there be questions? If you are part of a panel, when will you be called on? The more you know, the better shape you'll be in.
* Writing the Speech. Never go in without something in front of you to read from or, at least, glance at. I always write my speeches as if they were going to be printed. I type them triple-spaced on white paper, which means I have to wear glasses when I read them, but I prefer this to large block letters on cards. In writing, I always try for a warm or amusing beginning, a substantive middle, and an inspirational summing-up. Instead of trying to sound like Winston Churchill, I keep close to my own conversational style. Lectern trick I learned from President Ford: Place the page you're starting to read on the right, so that you have two sheets in front of you. Then you can maintain the natural flow as you move the next page from left to right.
* Dress the Part. If it's a black-tie dinner, go formal, of course. But don't overdress at a local luncheon unless you're narrating a fashion show. And don't turn up in something too casual at a traditional women's club. Your meeting chairman should be able to guide you.
* Check Out the Podium. If the lectern is too high, ask for a riser. If your mouth gets dry, be sure there's a glass of water handy. Check the mike and lectern lights ahead of time, too.
* Luncheons and Dinners. If there is a guest-of-honor reception, go early and move around—it's a great place for contacts. If you're sitting on the dais, remember not to chew with your mouth open or crumble your rolls nervously. If you're speaking after a meal, eat lightly and don't have more than one drink.
* Questions. Spontaneous queries from the floor aren't al-

214

ways forthcoming. Plant a few, or have some written out on cards you can pull out with the explanation "On the way to this seminar, I was asked . . ." Cut off foolish questions, but don't be rude about it.

* Speaker's Shakes. Don't feel exceptional if your knees buckle when you step up to the platform, and if your voice sounds as if it belongs to someone else. Even accomplished speakers get tense. Remedy: Breathe deeply, fix on one person in the front row, and speak as if there were just two of you in the room. When you get your balance, though, sweep your eyes across the entire audience.
* Relief and Rewards. There are moments of joy and release in everybody's life: coming down from the delivery room, leaving the doctor's office after an encouraging verdict, stepping on terra firma after a rough plane trip. And then there's that delicious moment when, with applause ringing in your ears, you pick up your text and sit down, knowing your speech was a hit. Enjoy.

P.S.—If you've received an award, don't leave it on the table, as I once did.

Enlarging the Circle

Still having the same tired old crowd to your parties? There's nothing wrong with good friends, but variety does add spice to social occasions, and even the most timid host or hostess can be daring once in a while.

If you're a single woman, it's "downright upright" to invite a man you don't know to your house or apartment, especially if you're having a group. Two women I know combined forces and lists from their respective files, and threw a black-tie dinner that hyped their social life for months to come.

If you and your mate are in an entertaining rut, don't stay there. My husband and I always mix medical and communications types; both sides love the fresh exposures. So does a celebrity, of whatever wattage. That author visiting your city on a tour, your congressman, or that controversial reporter from your local TV station could all probably be lured to a party by a note saying, "You won't know many people, but we're an interested group who would love to meet you informally. I promise, the food and wine will be good, and someone will pick you up and take you home."

Adopt people, too. Your child's teacher, your gym instructor, that foreign couple down the block, all would probably welcome an invitation. And don't scorn matchmaking, either, impromptu or forewarned. (Be careful of the prowlers, however. Never let it be said that a match made in heaven went to hell at your New Year's Eve party because you brought in a hunter or a huntress who zoomed in on your best friend's husband or wife. Or *yours*.)

Parties are for people. Nobody cares if you don't have Spode, Waterford, or Baccarat, or if you serve the wrong wine with the chicken, or even if you had all the food sent in. If the mix was good, and there was a lot of electricity and interchange, and some dancing in the aisles, and two people who didn't know each other found each other, and everybody went home in a good mood, you are on your way to establishing your hospitality reputation.

Icebreakers

A woman friend of mine at a dinner party was asked by the stranger on her right, "How many times have you been married?" "Twice," she answered, and he proceeded further. "Which husband did you like the best?" he asked.

Thanks to that presumptuous power serve, stranger on her right is well on his way to becoming Husband No. 3.

Not everybody is poised enough, or brash enough, or

quick enough, to dream up clever opening ploys with un-
familiar people at parties, meetings, dinners, luncheons,
and weddings. In fact, many people are wooden or inert
and thus miss out making new connections because they
can't think of what to say.

Here's my basic list of icebreaking gambits suitable for
use in a wide variety of situations. They're not as far out as
the man who saw his future famous ad-woman wife on a
railroad platform and approached her by asking, deadpan,
"Did you ever notice there aren't any blue M&M's?"

These openers are probably more reliable.

- Identification: Even if there are place cards or name tags,
  play it straight. "I'm Susy Smith. What's your name?"
  Unless you mean it, *not* that tired old "Haven't I seen you
  somewhere before?"

- Weather: "This kind of weather is good for something. I
  wonder what."

- Connection: "How do you happen to know ———?"
  (The host, the hostess, the bride, the groom, the speaker,
  or anybody else in the room.)

- Occupation: "What do you do? No, don't tell me. Let me
  guess."

- Personal: "Isn't that dress a Halston?" (Even if you saw it
  in Sears.)
  "What a handsome tie!" (If he isn't wearing one, move
  on to shirt.)
  "Did I see your name in Suzy's column?" (Everybody
  likes to be part of the millionaire mystique.)

- Sports: "You look like a (skier, runner, tennis player,
  football player, golfer, etc.) Do you play professionally?"

- News: "Did you hear Dan Rather on the news tonight?" "What do you think of the news?" Or "What do you think of Dan Rather?"

- Shared Confusion: "I don't recognize a person here. Have you any idea of what this is all about?"

- Action Ice Breakers:
  "I wonder if you'd get me a drink."
  "This kind of music always makes me want to dance."
  "Would you like to come back to my place for a nightcap?"

From then on, the ice gets thinner and you're on your own.

"Not Now, Honey, the Baby's Crying"

It was Hester Mundis' *Journal* article that rang many bells on the sex life of harried parents. Advice: "The best aphrodisiac for a marriage that has been overexposed to farina, nursery rhymes, tricycles, pediatricians, and tooth fairies is a baby sitter . . . And the right time should be any time you're in the mood, not just that Friday night out for dinner and the movies."

It is a paragraph I often quote, especially to new young parents. Keep those emergency numbers handy.

Business Is Business

You may hang your hat in the office, and stash an extra raincoat in the closet. But don't confuse the office with home, although many work-lovers do. I remember Charlotte Curtis of *The New York Times* telling a group of communications women that she felt comforted that the paper was open twenty-four hours a day, so she could go there and write whenever she felt the urge.

Sometimes we get too hooked on our jobs and the people who share them with us. Men, who largely think of business as a game, will seek camaraderie, but always maintain a competitive edge. Women, on the other hand, tend to get involved more intimately: sharing confidences, leaning on coworkers and supervisors for emotional support, acting out the roles of mother, daughter, sister, wife.

Office friendships (and office romances) sometimes seem to put your life in focus, add warmth and meaning to daily routines. But veterans like myself will also point out that such dependencies can get very, very sticky. Friendship falters when your dearest pal gets promoted over you. Rejection stings when your protector starts pushing for the new girl who came in last week. Or, from another point of view, when the protégé you've been grooming leaves you for a better job . . . or makes a hidden bid for yours.

I'm not suggesting that one should turn one's back on the bonds and attachments that arise in a work situation. I have made some strong friendships through my career, and many have persisted even though our situations changed.

Today, I miss having a large staff, not because of the sense of power but because of the constant stimulation of a work-family, the story-swapping, the joint appreciation of problems and details nobody outside would ever appreciate.

But industry today is more ephemeral than it ever was. I would warn a newcomer, especially a young woman executive on the way up, against getting too deeply involved on a personal level with anyone in the office, male or female. It is almost always a risk to your professional progress. And you can get hit in the heart as well as in the pay envelope.

Have lunch, share gossip, talk over the weekends, see each other outside. But keep a small zone of privacy and objectivity. Don't get socked in. The bottom line is always there: Business is business.

Internships on Magazines

College students (and their parents) often ask me how to get a summer job on a magazine. For college juniors with real interest in magazine journalism, the best program is the one sponsored by the American Society of Magazine Editors, with a grant from the Magazine Publishers Association. It's a 10-week course, with assignments at more than fifty magazines, and a standard stipend of $200 a week before deductions. Interns are responsible for their own travel expenses to New York as well as housing, but ASME can help make arrangements for inexpensive quarters.

The rub: This is the best program in the nation—about a hundred former interns are now working on magazines. But it's highly competitive in the selection of candidates. For further information, write Robert E. Kenyon, Jr., at the American Society of Magazine Editors, 575 Lexington Avenue, New York, N.Y. 10022.

The Listening Lack

At home or in the office, with your lover or your boss or your children, you'll get a lot further if you're a good listener.

Someone once told me that all of the women in the Kennedy family were schooled in the art of adroit listening. If you drew one of them as a dinner partner, she would fix her attentive gaze on you, and react as if every word you uttered were fascinating and significant.

Like many other busy people, I tend to be impatient. I want everybody to give me the message in "elevator speech," condensed so it can be absorbed between the twentieth and the ground floor. But I've disciplined myself *not* to be:

* A Flitter: Always willing to break up a conversation to take a phone call, or eavesdrop on that exchange at the next table, or between those VIPs on the other side of the room.
* A Quitter: Tuning out or walking away when someone says "It's a long story," interrupting when I see the point of an argument several minutes before it's been stated.
* A Monopolizer: Telling *my* jokes or anecdotes before everyone else because I think they're funnier, giving *my* opinions on the news because I think they're wiser, or maybe because the sound of my own voice makes me feel more secure in a roomful of strange people.

I must admit, however, that I have a tendency to listen to things unsaid, and to be sensitive to the nonverbal cues people send out. "All right," as an answer to "How are things?" can have many shades of meaning, from delightful to dire. I can sometimes answer the telephone and tell from a friend's "Hello" that there's a major problem, just by the tone of voice.

In these days of increasing electronic input, when we're picking up signals from transponders and walking around with earplugs in our ears, isn't it a good idea to fine-tune more on what *people* around you are saying? And don't just listen (although sometimes silence is indicated). React, respond, and most of all, *care*.

Bicoastal Dining

I am a restaurant freak; love to read about them, love to eat in them. I have lots of favorites all over the country, ranging from inexpensive ethnic cafés to the most *luxe*, but here are my *crème de la crème* selections in New York and Los Angeles.

Warning: the prices throughout are steep.

The Four Seasons: 99 East 52 Street (212–754–9494)
Maybe it's because I have "my table" in the Pool Room, and because Tom Margittai and Paul Kovi even included my signature in their cookbook. But I think not. This is generally considered the best all-around restaurant in New York: gracious, roomy, with wonderful food, a great wine list, and a famed dessert wagon. The Grill Room at lunch is filled with publishing types; at night, it features an after-theater menu. There's a pre-theater menu in the Pool Room that's slightly less expensive. If you have but one shoot-the-wallet restaurant to visit in New York, this is it. Reserve well ahead.

Russian Tea Room: 150 West 57 Street (212–265–0947)
Owned by a woman, Faith Stewart-Gordon, this festive restaurant is next to Carnegie Hall, serves blini, borscht, shashlik and other Russian dishes. Mostly, you go for the festive ambiance, and to celebrity-watch. Here gather the most prestigious doers and shakers in show business, media and culture worlds, especially at lunch. (Make your reservation before you come to town.)

IN LOS ANGELES

Breakfast:
Don Hernando in the Beverly Wilshire Hotel. Huevos rancheros, corned beef hash, bagels and lox, and everybody making deals.

Lunch:
The Bistro Garden: 176 North Canon Drive, Beverly

Hills (213–550–3900)
A sunny garden with wonderful salads, beautiful suntanned people, and everybody making deals. Reservations necessary.

Dinner:
La Scala: 9455 Little Santa Monica Boulevard, Beverly
Hills (213–275–0579)
Italian food magnifico, lots of stars, even bigger deals
over the veal marsala. Reserve early.

L'Ermitage: 730 N. La Cienega Blvd. L.A. (213–652
–5840)
French food fantastique. Here, they're probably swapping
studios over the duck breast in Médoc. Reserve early and
drop an important name.

Stay Out of the Slush

So you think you can write, and you'd like to see your by-
line in a big magazine. Before you invest time and money
and send a manuscript on its way (too often without keeping a carbon copy!) listen to the voice of reality. *Ladies' Home
Journal* receives more than 18,000 queries a year. *They buy
120.* That's less than 1 percent.

The 17,880 rejects are largely unsolicited submissions
which land in a pile called "slush," to be read by juniors or
free-lancers, who save time by a quick weeding of the ama-
teurish, the trite, the inappropriate, or the otherwise impossible. In the case of special features or contests in which
submissions are invited, there is a more careful screening.

As a starting writer, how do you get up there in the class
of Linda Wolfe, Susan Edmiston, Cliff Jahr, Ann Roiphe,
Maggie Scarfe, Susan Jacoby, and other big free-lance mag-

azine writers who make upward of $3,000 an article? It isn't easy, but it can happen.

You might begin by writing to the American Society of Journalists and Authors (ASJA), the nationwide organization of nonfiction writers, with a membership of about 600 free-lancers. They will send you information on their group, and for $1, a guidelines brochure on the unwritten code of ethics operating between editors and authors. (Write ASJA, 1501 Broadway, Suite 1907, New York, N.Y. 10036) They will also tell you about their annual writers' conference, and about helpful books on magazine writing.

Then there's a trade magazine called *Writer's Digest,* which carries many pertinent articles, marketing tips, and news and ads for writers' conferences all around the country. These usually are held during the summer, at universities, and are usually staffed by working editors and writers. (Be sure you review the faculties and facilities carefully and check out the fees and curriculum before you sign up for one of these courses.)

Of course you can study the market yourself—not just the big magazines, but smaller ones, too. What is the style, length, and approach these publications seem to prefer? Do they emphasize small, quick items or deeply researched service pieces? Is there a demand for first-person narratives, ordeal stories? These are always a good way to break in—especially through such features as *Redbook*'s Young Mother's Story.

You have a great idea that's just right for a specific publication. What do you do?

Don't send a manuscript. Prepare a proposal, sometimes called a query letter. Make sure it is crisp, concise, cleanly typed, and well phrased. Add your name, address, writing credits if you have them, and one or two clippings that prove you have put words together before. Don't automatically mail this to the top editor. Pick a name further on down the mast-head—articles editor, features editor, health and beauty editor, etc. You'll get more attention. And always enclose a self-addressed stamped envelope, for good news or bad.

Best bet: Work through a literary agent
The harsh reality: Very few established agents are willing to take on nonfiction (or fiction) writers unless they are major published names. It helps to have written a book, so maybe start at the top. Resource: *Inside Publishing,* by Bill Adler (my agent), Bobbs-Merrill. It tells you everything you need to know about book publishing, in case you have a best seller in your system. For a list of agents, try the annual *Literary Market Place,* published by R.R. Bowker Company, 1180 Avenue of the Americas, New York, N.Y. 10036. Or your local library. Overall advice: Don't give up at the first few rejection slips. Keep reading, keep writing, and keep in the swim. If you're good enough, and determined enough, you'll get published.

"I know I drink a lot, but I can't stop."
"There is nothing to live for anymore."
"I hate everybody, including myself."
"I have this terrible phobia."
"My marriage is on the rocks."
"I can't cope with that child another minute."
There are times in everybody's life when the pressures mount and the stress gets intolerable. Sometimes it is a pass-ing response to normal crises. But often the painful symptoms signal a real mental health problem, for which professional help is indicated.

Women's magazines have done an important job in reassur-ing readers that there is nothing weak, shameful, or mysteri-ous about seeking psychiatric therapy when it is needed. I

225

myself have sought treatment at two points when the world seemed to be crumbling, and both times, I was fully productive and upbeat within a short period. Psychotherapy is no magic cure. For many devout believers, prayer and faith are the ultimate prescription.

But if you, or a member of your family, are in deep trouble, *get help*. Try your family doctor, your local mental health clinic, social service agencies, or your religious adviser. But don't wait until you break down. Reach for support *before* you fall.

The Male Robot

Last year, when I came home from an exhilarating and educational trip to Japan, I sat around with a bunch of young women in the office discussing the whole new trend to robots.

"Wouldn't it be great," asked one of the swingier singles, "if they could invent a male robot that would save us all the trouble of hanging around bars, health clubs, and all the other places you are supposed to meet what they call men these days?"

"Provided we could program it," added one of the girls who worked with computers. I asked for a list, and after filing some of the most raunchy comments, here's how the group saw the opportunity.

THE PERFECT MALE ROBOT

* It wouldn't tell you it liked you better with long hair.
* It would never ask you "Am I the first?" "Am I the best?" "How was I?"
* It would never leave the toilet seat up.
* It would not say, "I'll call you a cab."
* It would not have to go home to its wife on Christmas and holidays.

* It would never say, "I am not the marrying kind."
* It would not leave its hair on the sink.
* It wouldn't have sex hangups.
* It wouldn't care if it made less money than you do.
* It would offer to cook dinner once in a while.
* It wouldn't care if you were a virgin.
* It wouldn't care if you weren't a virgin.
* It wouldn't make you enumerate all your past lovers.
* It would *listen.*
* It would be able to say, with simplicity and sincerity, "I love you."

"The problem is," wrote one young woman on the bottom of her list, "if it were *that* perfect, you'd know it was a robot. And eventually, you'd find yourself becoming one, too."

When Giving Is Gaining

One of the disagreements I have had with radical feminists is their attitude toward volunteerism. "Don't give it away!" warned early posters. True, there is some merit in the argument that women sometimes donate services that deserve a salary. But many women would prefer to work in a hospital rather than play bridge. And others are learning that volunteerism is a good way to learn new skills and expand contacts.

In my case, I always found that I gained more than I gave when I worked on various causes and served on the boards of nonprofit groups such as the Riverdale Neighborhood House, New York Girl Scouts, Women's Forum, and the National Committee for Prevention of Child Abuse. There's always the pleasing sense of paying your dues, and the knowledge that you are helping to make it a better world. But there's also a growth factor as you watch powerful people in action and learn a lot about project-planning, budgeting, and other management techniques.

How do you get on the board of a nonprofit or charitable organization? Yes, you are often invited because of your clout, your skills, or your access to big donors. But there are other paths, from the inside up. First, of course, you have to join. Then you volunteer for committees, work your head off, and get noticed for your enthusiasm and effectiveness. If you let it be known that you're anxious to go further, it could happen.

The trick, of course, is to pick a group that needs you, and one that matches your interests. Caution: Don't sign yourself up for a commitment you can't handle. Board members and committee chairs really have to show for meetings, and really have to sell those benefit tickets.

Incidentally, once you get a reputation as a good board member, other groups will seek you out. Never underestimate the exhilaration factor in volunteer recognition. It is almost as heady as career achievement!

ELEVEN

Open Ender

"O! In the virgin womb of the imagination the word was made flesh," wrote Joyce. Other literary minds have also drawn the comparison between the gestation and labor preceding the birth of a child, and of a book.

Comfortingly, this book's pages have finally fattened to a viable bulk in its cardboard cradle, the *de rigueur* empty typewriting-paper box. No amniocentesis is available for tidings of best-seller potential. Nevertheless, I must let go.

From friends who have been there, I have received warnings. Along with buoyant relief, I am told, postpartum depression sweeps in. Expectantly, I face freer weekends, knowing that I now can clean up those mountains of papers in the bedroom, resume some lapsed relationships, get to a few chaotic closets.

But what will replace The Book as a voracious devourer of time? For what will stories be clipped from newspapers, apt phrases stored, notes made by flashlight in the middle of the night so as not to disturb a sleeping husband?

Already I am lonely. Not yet in the delivery room, already I plan a sibling.

Around me through this busy year at the typewriter, the

world has been careening. The months have been crammed with work, change, tension, and drama. In the larger scheme of things, the news from all fronts has been mostly heavy and dark. In my own orbit, sunlight and shadows have intermingled.

In 1981, I left the *Journal* to head up a development company which was to be largely devoted to TV, cable, and other electronic media. Like the *Journal*, it was part of a major American conglomerate, the Charter Company, based in Jacksonville and headed by an extraordinary man named Raymond K. Mason.

I faced the challenge excitedly, reaching for new dimensions. Projects were conceived, planned, and launched. With my good friend Lucy Jarvis, the celebrated TV producer, I worked on a major TV special, "Family Reunion," starring Bette Davis. It ran in prime time on two subsequent nights on NBC, and collected good ratings and a few awards. Other shows, for cable and network, were in the hopper, poised for production.

Then, for a complex set of reasons, Charter decided to sell its two magazines, *Ladies' Home Journal* and *Redbook,* and to dissolve the rest of its communications holdings. This meant the closing out of many jobs for reasons having nothing to do with the talents or the abilities of the people forced to leave.

In late July 1982, four top Charter executives—men I knew and respected—were killed in Ireland in a devastating helicopter crash, as they flew from a business meeting in Ballynahinch Castle, north Galway, to the airport in Shannon, where they were to take a plane to Paris.

The accident was a stunning blow to all of us, another reminder of how frail is the fabric of human existence, how ruthlessly chance cancels our calculations, how the subterranean mystery of life and the inevitable secret of death lies beneath our daily routine, but how we must necessarily embrace life and move forward.

Because of the business changes, my own operation was compelled to taper off and prepare for close-down. Existing projects, in various stages of development, had to be handed over to the new owners of the magazines. I stayed on with the parent company, Charter, where I am now a consultant on special projects. But I also have the freedom to pursue other interests.

Luckily, I have been no stranger to upheaval and transition. Nothing remains the same, nor should it be static. People, relationships, properties, all have seasons, all must evolve to meet adjusted circumstances. Magazines, too, have cycles. *Newsweek* has acquired a new editor, *Rolling Stone* has moved from rock to broader issues, *Psychology Today* has been revamped. Virtually every long-established magazine is being looked at appraisingly by managements convinced that restatement and invigoration are the right ways to stay alive in a tough economy, with hard-hitting competition both from print and the electronic media.

Vigorous, strategy-wise Myrna Blyth, my successor, stays on with *Ladies' Home Journal* as editor. She is turning out a fast-paced product crammed with information and service, crisply in tune with today's market evaluations. I believe we view each other with mutual professional admiration. Although, when we lunch, we often end up talking about clothes, children, and gossip.

It may sound like a message on a floral wreath when I say I wish the *Journal* nothing but luck in the future. But *après moi le déluge* has never been my style. Too significant a part of me has been invested in the championship seasons of *Ladies' Home Journal* to want to see it fade, or be anything but a triumphant success . . . reader-wise and profit-wise. Economics, of course, is the key word as rumors persist that "The Seven Sisters," the women's magazines, are in trouble these days.

They are pressured, yes. Most of the badmouthing comes from cynics on Madison Avenue, who buy advertising by computer and by trendiness, who tend to think of anyone over thirty-five as a dowager, and anyone beyond city lines as a tea-party type from Dubuque.

To both readers and advertisers, the mass women's magazines offer the boons of scope and variety as opposed to the narrower subjects and concentrated markets in the so-called "specialty books." (Any day we'll have "Working Aunts," "The Transsexual Executive," or "Sloth: The Magazine for the Vibrant Non-Exerciser." Or am I already treading on someone's franchise?)

If I had any kibitzing advice for planners of women's magazines, it would be to urge a greater emphasis on importance and depth. I'm not saying we need any more caped crusaders, or heavy messages. I just feel that the next wave in American style will be a step beyond fast facts into more penetrating wisdom, that substance will come into its own again. And along with it, a reverence for graphic and literary quality.

"I bought the *Journal*," says Bob Riordan, its new owner who obtained part of his working capital from the Women's Bank, "because I believed this magazine has one of the greatest names and strongest reputations in the world. The *Journal* will celebrate its hundredth anniversary next year, but there's still a long run ahead." Bob, as I have said, is a marathon man, so he'll undoubtedly go the distance.

During this past year, I have learned a good deal about electronic media and high-tech. One of the most interesting experiences: working with CBS and AT&T on a videotex experiment, which was tested this past year in Ridgewood, New Jersey. To me, videotex seems to have the clearest shot at either replacing or synergistically supplementing newspapers

and magazines. Imagine, a single machine in your home—
AT&T is secretly betting it will replace the telephone—which
will provide you with your own tailored package of news,
information, recipes, shopping and banking facilities, and interactive communications with friends and business associates
all over the world. Preparing a program for videotex was a
fresh editorial experience: techspeak in some ways goes
against my grain. But I mastered it, and it is possibly something I will explore further.

I may also build on my adventures in the fast-churn
maelstrom of TV. Even after a short exposure, I am confident
enough to believe I can come up with some more fascinating,
audience-pleasing concepts than most of the mediocrities I see
on the tube. It's a sad day when commercials have more
inventiveness, verve, and impact than the programs.

There have been other eye-opening perspectives, too.

This past summer, shortly after the helicopter accident, I
too was in Ballynahinch Castle in Ireland, attending a small
but instructive conference of foundation executives, gathered
to discuss the future of private philanthropy in the health
field.

One of the liveliest guests was petite Eppie Lederer (Ann
Landers), whose perky personality and razor-sharp common
sense almost stole the show. (Eppie was also possibly the only
woman in history to sashay into a gregarious but grungy Irish
pub swathed in a chinchilla stole. The ghillies recovering from
a hard day catching salmon all thought she was wearing local
rabbit.)

Eppie, in that flat Sioux City, Iowa, twang, dispenses candid advice to bigwigs with the same insouciance she uses with
readers. Don't just take heed of the formal grant requests and
the big proposals, she told foundation executives who control
billions; listen to the anguish and the needs of little people, she
urged, reflecting much of the human sensitivity she exhibits in

her syndicated column. I was pleased to hear that Eppie also has advisory positions on such boards as the Harvard Medical School and the Menninger Foundation.

I watched her, bouncy and as filled with energy as a teen-ager. She is seemingly unscarred by the breakup of her thirty-six-year marriage, apparently forgiving of her twin sister, Popo (columnist Abby van Buren), who said all those mean things about Eppie in a recent issue of the *Journal*. As we talked, I polished my conviction that the secret of staying young is to stay current and involved, to accept no fixed or final stages in the flow of the human process, and to keep your motor running. As with Eppie, to me the term "retirement" is a ten-letter dirty word.

I don't know how the whole phenomenon of women's emer-gence will work out, although the facts of life are that we are going to live longer. Women in the work force will continue to be a major factor. But will female control really penetrate those upper levels where the real power lies? Men seem to be happy with the paycheck part of the two-paycheck marriage, and some fathers are pitching in with parenting. But down deep, have they really acknowledged equal partnership? Will they share housework, relocate cheerfully along with wives' reassignments in other cities, give up their centuries-old tradi-tion of dominance? Will knowing how to use our sex muscles and the mechanics of masturbation and oral sex bring us any closer to lasting love, or for that matter, even satisfying plea-sure? Will our Baskin-Robbins society, with its thirty flavors of everything, 100 TV channels, and options everywhere, help us get what we want—or just make us more insecure than ever about having to make up our minds?

I'm not answering these questions, just asking them. And relying on the future to sort them out.

"It does not do to leave a dragon out of your calculations if you live near one," wrote J.R.R. Tolkien.

I can hear some dragons breathing out there. In the inevitable changing of the guard in today's publishing world, some of my fellow editors face change reluctantly, fearing a sense of loss if their assignments change. Helen Gurley Brown, talking about leaving *Cosmo* at some future date, has stated that she's afraid she won't be invited to parties anymore. (A most unlikely prospect.)

Of course I miss being editor of a major magazine—the clout, the excitement, the deadlines, the discounts. But not as much as I thought I would. Beverly Sills has a charm which reads "I've already done that," and it is about how I feel when I look back.

My future, as is the case with many others, now requires an attitude of *responsive flexibility*. I stole this concept from an irrepressible friend of mine, Cathy Cash Spellman, whose big novel *So Many Partings* will be published this year. It is a romantic epic that is like a Gaelic *Gone With the Wind*.

Cathy, whose flowing, fiery-red hair can be seen from a block away, and whose intuitive vitality can warm you for days, has a highly successful cosmetics business, but many other strings to her bow. She's encountered some overpowering dragons in her life, to be sure. But her optimistic fighting spirit has turned them back.

"If you build your security deep within you, you will need fewer security blankets," she once wrote to her daughters.

People chase the goddess of success in all her guises: love, money, fame, power, possessions. They are all nice to have, but they are all perishable. If one section of your structure collapses, or the whole roof falls in, you must have the responsive flexibility to build substitute housing for dreams and ambitions. And you should never, never go rummaging among the ruins for proof that it was the architect's fault, not yours.

"You're not growing older, you're getting better" may not sound like an accurate slogan on a morning when your knees creak and there's a whole new network of lines around your eyes in the bathroom mirror.

But it still has merit. My old resource, Emerson, says it: "People wish to be settled; only as far as they are unsettled is there hope for them."

I have this deep-seated hunch that if I keep a cocked eye for opportunity, my appetite for adventure and enthusiasm high, my sense of humor activated, and a net out for the future, there are some sensational things ahead.

Under the sheets or between the covers, it hasn't been bad for openers. I wonder what will turn up next.

Index

Index

238

Index

Index